Peterson
First Guide

to

SHELLS

of North America

Jackie Leatherbury Douglass

Illustrations by
John Douglass

HOUGHTON
MIFFLIN
COMPANY
•
BOSTON
NEW YORK

Copyright © 1989 by Houghton Mifflin Company
Editor's Note copyright © 1989 by Roger Tory Peterson

For information about permission to reproduce selections from
this book, write to trade.permissions@hmco.com or to
Permissions, Houghton Mifflin Harcourt Publishing Company,
3 Park Avenue, 19th Floor, New York, New York 10016.

www.hmhco.com

PETERSON FIRST GUIDES,
PETERSON FIELD GUIDES and
PETERSON FIELD GUIDE SERIES
are registered trademarks of
Houghton Mifflin Company.

Selected illustrations and text reproduced from *A Field
Guide to Shells Coloring Book* Copyright © 1985 by
Houghton Mifflin Company

Library of Congress Cataloging-in-Publication Data

Douglass, Jackie Leatherbury.
Peterson first guide to shells of North America.

Includes index.
1. Shells—North America—Identification.
I. Douglass, John.   II. Title.   III. Title: Shells of
North America.
QL411.D68   1989   594'.0471'097   88-32884
ISBN 0-395-91182-6

Printed in China

SCP 32 31 30 29 28 27 26 25 24

4500789412

Editor's Note

In 1934, my *Field Guide to the Birds* first saw the light of day. This book was designed so that live birds could be readily identified at a distance, by their patterns, shapes, and field marks, without resorting to the technical points specialists use to name species in the hand or in the specimen tray. The book introduced the "Peterson System," as it is now called, a visual system based on patternistic drawings with arrows to pinpoint the key field marks. The system is now used throughout the Peterson Field Guide Series, which has grown to over thirty-five volumes on a wide range of subjects, from ferns to fishes, shells to stars, and animal tracks to edible plants.

Even though Peterson Field Guides are intended for the novice as well as the expert, there are still many beginners who would like something simpler to start with — a smaller guide that would give them confidence. It is for this audience — those who perhaps recognize a crow or a robin, a buttercup or a daisy, but little else — that the Peterson First Guides have been created. They offer a selection of the animals and plants you are most likely to see during your first forays afield. By narrowing the choices — and using the Peterson System — they make identification much easier. First Guides make it easy to get started in the field, and easy to graduate to the full-fledged Peterson Field Guides.

Roger Tory Peterson

Introducing the Shells

Shells come in an infinite variety of elegant shapes and patterns. Each one is a natural sculpture, a piece of fine art. Some shells are smooth and polished, with pure, fine-lined shapes. Others are covered with bumpy ridges or knobs or sharp spines that we can't resist touching. The colors of shells are most fascinating; they are especially luscious when the shell is wet. It is no wonder that so many people enjoy collecting shells.

Although most of the shells we find along the shore are empty, each one once contained an animal called a mollusk. The mollusks make up one of the largest groups in the animal kingdom, second only to the insects. There are 150,000 mollusks, including both fossils and living animals. About half of them are marine mollusks, which means that they live in the ocean, usually inside seashells.

Mollusks are cold-blooded animals with soft bodies. They are unsegmented and have no internal skeleton. The animal's shell, formed of limy material secreted by a fleshy mantle covering the body, serves as its skeleton. The shell supports the body and provides shelter, including protection from predators. Some mollusks, such as slugs, do not have shells. Shells help mollusks survive conditions ranging from desert heat that reaches 112° Fahrenheit to the icy cold waters of frozen ponds or arctic seas.

Some of the marine mollusks live offshore, just below the surface water on the high seas, or at depths of up to 3 miles, where they are under great pressure. Others live in relatively shallow water near shore, often in the intertidal zone between the high- and low-tide lines. The empty shells of these animals have usually been worn down or battered by the surf by the time they wash ashore, but even these old, chipped or faded shells can be beautiful. A mollusk's shell is never shed while the animal is alive. As the animal grows, new limy shell material is added to the edge of the aperture (opening) of the shell. Like the growth rings in

a tree's trunk, the shell material records the life history, from birth to death, of the animal that lives inside.

Some mollusks — the bivalves (see p. 78) — have 2 paired shells that can open and close. The clams, oysters, mussels, and scallops belong to this group. The gastropods (see p. 6), a large group including the conchs, limpets, cones, and many other marine snails, usually have a single shell. The scaphopods (see p. 120) also have only one shell, which is shaped like a hollow tube or elephant's tusk. The chitons (see p. 74) have a single armored shell, which consists of 8 plates held together by muscles and a surrounding tough, leathery girdle. The cephalopods (see p. 124) — the squids, octopuses, and their relatives — generally have no external shell, although some of them have a hardened internal blade or "pen."

A shell usually consists of 3 major layers. The outer layer, which is often thin and flaky, is called the periostracum. This "skin" protects the shell from chemicals in the water or air. Next is the thicker, more colorful middle layer called the prismatic layer. The smooth inner layer of a shell is called the nacreous layer. It is this iridescent layer of mother-of-pearl that gives the shells of abalones and other mollusks a beautiful interior.

In this *First Guide to Shells* you will find a small sample of the 70,000 species of marine mollusks that live off North America's seacoasts. Like other guides in the Peterson First Guide series, this is a simplified handbook for beginners, not a complete guide for experts. To encourage interest in shells and to help identify shells for collecting, I have selected the most colorful, not necessarily the most common, shells for this book. The size given in the descriptions refers to the length of the shell when the animal is mature.

GASTROPODS
(UNIVALVES AND OTHERS)

Gastropods are the largest class of mollusks, with 50,000 or more species in the world. There are about 7,000 species in North America. Gastropod fossils have been found that date back 500 million years. Sixty percent of the gastropods are snails that live in seawater. The rest live in fresh water or on land.

The word gastropod means "stomach-footed." Most of the snails in this group crawl about on a large, muscular foot that protrudes from their shells. Some have a horny or shelly operculum, or "trap door," on the back of the foot (see p. 7). In case of danger, the snail withdraws into its shell and closes the opening with the operculum.

Most of these snails are univalves, meaning that they have only one shell. A univalve usually stays in the same spiral shell for its whole life.

In univalves the mantle, which is shaped like a hood or cape, lines the shell and helps protect the animal's soft body. Glands in the mantle secrete a sticky fluid that hardens into the limy shell material. In some species, such as the cowries (p. 56) and the marginellas (p. 58), the mantle extends like a curtain, wholly or partly covering the shell and protecting it. The mantle is often brightly colored.

A typical univalve can feel, smell, and taste. In the mantle cavity of the animal, there is a head with eyes, one or two tentacles, and a snout or proboscis with a mouth. A ribbonlike organ called the radula is used to obtain and tear food; it may have many rows of sharp teeth. All gastropods have a digestive system and a heart. They breathe through gills or through a single gill located behind the heart.

Univalve shells are extremely variable in shape: some are long, slender spirals; others are cap-shaped. Each shell has an opening called the aperture, with edges called lips. Univalve shells vary in size from large

to microscopic, and their exterior may be sculptured or plain. Some gastropods — the slugs that live on land and the nudibranchs, or sea slugs — have no shell at all.

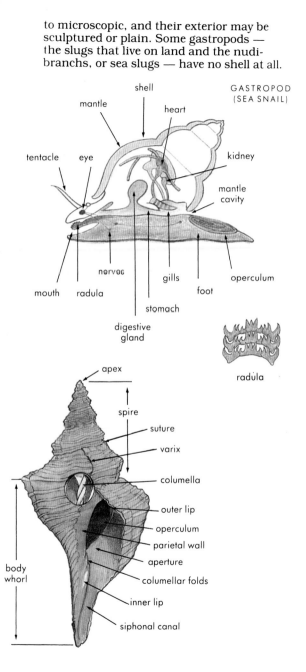

GASTROPOD (SEA SNAIL)

shell
mantle
heart
tentacle
eye
kidney
mantle cavity
mouth
radula
nerves
gills
foot
operculum
stomach
digestive gland

radula

apex
spire
suture
varix
columella
outer lip
operculum
parietal wall
aperture
columellar folds
inner lip
siphonal canal
body whorl

GASTROPODS: CARRIER SHELLS

Four carrier shells are found in North American waters — 3 in the Atlantic off the U.S. and one off the Pacific Coast of Mexico.

A carrier shell is fairly thin and cone-shaped (wider than it is high), and twisted in a spiral, like a winding staircase. The underside of the shell is flattened.

The scientific name for the carrier shells comes from Greek words meaning "bearing strangers," which describes the way carrier shells conceal themselves from predators. The snail that lives inside each shell secretes a sticky substance and cements empty shells or stones to the upperside of the shell. This may reinforce the shell as well as disguise it. Seen from above, the shell looks like a mound of broken shells or a small pile of rocks or other debris. Only the underside of the shell reveals the snail's true identity.

Carrier shells camouflage themselves using materials that reflect their surroundings: they use shells in areas with shells on the bottom, and they use stones when the bottom is rocky. They rarely mix objects. In deep, murky water where the need for concealment is not so great, there are few objects on the shell.

The snails that live in carrier shells are active animals that feed on algae (seaweed) and detritus (decaying plant and animal matter and inorganic debris that sinks to the bottom). They move by sending out their large muscular foot, thrusting the thorny operculum ("trap door") of the shell into the mud or sand, and flipping forward.

ATLANTIC CARRIER SHELL   1–3 in.

Found on sandy bottoms in shallow water or in mud and silt in deeper water, from North Carolina to Brazil.

upperside

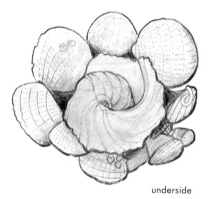

underside

ATLANTIC CARRIER SHELL

GASTROPODS: CONCHS

Conchs are also known as strombs. Of the 7 species of winged conchs in the tropical Atlantic region, only 3 reach Florida. None of the 4 Pacific Coast species is found farther north than the Gulf of California.

Mature conchs have a thick, solid, heavy shell with a U-*shaped indentation* on the lower end of the outer lips. This is known as the stromboid notch. When a living snail is inside the shell, its right eye sticks out of this notch. The "*wing*," a large, greatly flaring outer lip, is as high or higher than the spire in some species such as the Roostertail and Hawk-wing conchs. The pointed spire almost always has knobs or spines on the last 2 whorls. The shell is covered with a thin periostracum (skin) that flakes off easily when the shell is dry.

Conchs move by stabbing their sharp, thorny, clawlike operculum into the sand and tumbling over. The operculum, or trap door, is also used to ward off enemies.

See also p. 12.

QUEEN CONCH   8–12 in.

Also known as the Pink Conch or Queen Stromb. The young of this harmless conch, called "rollers," are so similar in shape to poisonous cone snails (see p. 38) that they can sometimes fool shell collectors. Adult females sometimes weigh more than 5 lbs. (Females are usually larger than males.)

This conch, which is delicious to eat, occasionally produces pink pearls. The shell is used to make cameos and porcelain. It is found from southeastern Florida to the West Indies.

ROOSTER-TAIL CONCH   4–7 in.

Found from southeastern Florida to the West Indies.

HAWK-WING CONCH   1¾–6 in.

Found from southeastern Florida to Brazil.

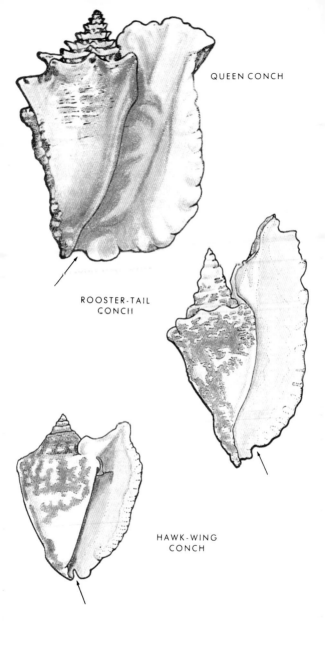

QUEEN CONCH

ROOSTER-TAIL
CONCH

HAWK-WING
CONCH

GASTROPODS: CONCHS, *continued*

Conchs are large, plant-eating snails that feed on delicate green algae (seaweed). They live mostly in shallow grassy areas of warm seas.

MILK CONCH   4–7 in.

This shell is covered with fine spiral lines and has low knobs on the spire. It is found on sand among seagrass in shallow water, from Florida to the West Indies.

FLORIDA FIGHTING CONCH   2¾–5 in.

The winglike outer lip is low and slopes *downward*. The spire has short blunt spines. This conch is found on sandy mud among seagrass, from North Carolina to Texas.

WEST INDIAN FIGHTING CONCH   3–5 in.

The shell has an *upward-sloping outer lip* and long spines on its short spire. An active snail, found in shallow water from southern Florida to the West Indies and south to Brazil.

GASTROPODS: CROWN CONCHS

There are 25 species of crown conchs worldwide. Eleven are found in our shallow tropical seas, in waters ranging from brackish to salty. These relatively large snails are scavengers but also feed on live mollusks. As in the conchs (above), the shells of the females are usually larger than those of the males. The shell has a large body whorl with a conical spire. The aperture is protected by an oval, clawlike operculum.

FLORIDA CROWN CONCH   3–5 in.

This shell has a high spire with one or more rows of *open spines* on the shoulder. It is found in shallow quiet water, from Florida to Brazil.

MILK
CONCH

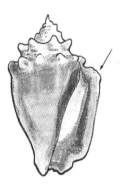

FLORIDA
FIGHTING
CONCH

WEST
INDIAN
FIGHTING
CONCH

FLORIDA
CROWN
CONCH

GASTROPODS: HELMET SHELLS

Of the 60 species of helmets worldwide, 11 species live in North American temperate and tropical climes, in shallow to moderately deep waters.

These beautiful, medium- to giant-sized shells are solid, with large body whorls, *short spires*, and *knobs*. Every few whorls, a ridge called a varix marks the place where the outer lip used to be. The actual outer lip is prominent and usually thickened. There are teeth on either side of the narrow aperture. The aperture is protected by a thin, horny operculum. A highly polished, richly colored, broad *parietal shield* (the area opposite the outer lip) covers the part of the shell that rests on the foot. The *siphonal canal*, which is short but well developed, is curved upward at its very end.

Helmet snails creep over sandy sea bottoms, using their large foot. They have tentacles, which are used for touching. The eyes are situated at the base of these feelers. Helmets are carnivores (meat-eaters); they eat mostly sea urchins.

Helmet shells have been used for centuries by man: as food (the snails are delicious in chowder), as scoops to bail out boats, and as cups and cooking pots (halved, with the core of the shell removed). They have also been used as trumpets. These thick shells have many layers of variable and interesting colors that make them desirable to cut into cameos, for jewelry.

KING HELMET   4–9 in.
Found in shallow water, from North Carolina to Brazil.

FLAME HELMET   3–4 in.
There are brown spots between the top teeth of this helmet, but *none* between the *bottom teeth*. This shell is found in shallow water, from southern Florida to Brazil.

HORNED HELMET   To 12 in.
Found in deep water around Hawaii.

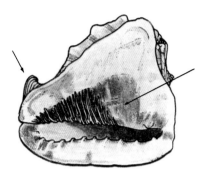

KING HELMET

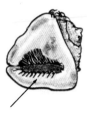

FLAME
HELMET

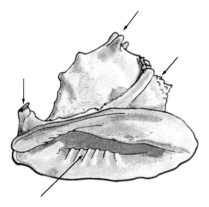

HORNED
HELMET

GASTROPODS: BONNETS

Bonnets belong to the helmet family (see p. 14). They have many features in common with other helmets, but they are smaller and lack a large, solid parietal shield and an upturned siphonal canal. A *pimpled callus* often covers the parietal wall opposite the outer lip, which is toothed and thickened. The male snail's shell is shorter than the female's. Like most female helmets, female bonnets lay a tower of eggs encased in capsules. The larvae (young) are believed to be able to swim on their own when they emerge.

SCOTCH BONNET   1–3⅝ in.
This bonnet has weak spiral grooves and sometimes circles, which give the shell surface a slightly beaded effect. The Scotch Bonnet is the official shell for the state of North Carolina. It is found on sand in shallow water, from North Carolina to the Gulf of Mexico and south to Brazil.

SMOOTH SCOTCH BONNET   1½–2 in.
This shell is a variety of the Scotch Bonnet (above). It is smooth except for the rough *parietal shield*. This bonnet is found from southern Florida to Bermuda and south to Brazil.

GASTROPODS: TUN SHELLS

There are 4 North American species of this small family, including 2 in Florida. Twenty or so species exist worldwide, mainly in tropical seas.

The name tun shell means "cask shell" or "wine jar." These broadly inflated shells are rather thin and light but strong. The surface is sculptured with spiral lines and may be covered with a thin periostracum (skin). The outer lip is slightly thickened. The aperture is large, with a *deep siphonal canal* at the base, and there is no operculum. The animal is larger than the shell it lives in.

The snails that live in tun shells are carnivores. The snail's snout contains acid,

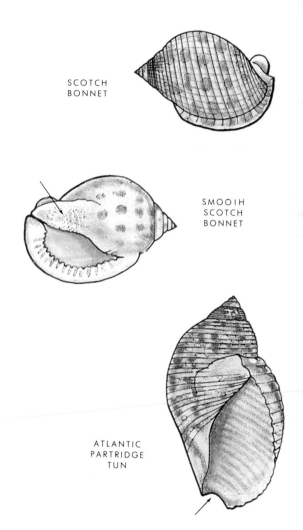

SCOTCH
BONNET

SMOOTH
SCOTCH
BONNET

ATLANTIC
PARTRIDGE
TUN

which helps it digest the bivalves (see p. 78) and sea cucumbers on which it feeds.

ATLANTIC PARTRIDGE TUN 1½–5¼ in.
This tun is found in sand in shallow water, from southeastern Florida to Brazil.

GASTROPODS: FROG SHELLS

Seven of the 30 or so species of this small tropical family are found in North America.

Frog shells are rather flattened, with a *distinct siphon canal* at both the *upper and lower ends* of the oval-shaped *aperture.* The inner and outer lips are generally ridged or toothed. The deep-water species in this group have sharp, blade-like ridges opposite each other, while the rock- and reef-dwelling frog shells have dull, knoblike ridges.

The animals that live inside these shells are carnivores (meat-eaters); they feed on marine worms and bivalves.

ST. THOMAS FROG SHELL   ¼–½ in.
Best known for its unusual oval-shaped lavender throat (aperture), and the *3 rounded knobs* between the ridges (varices) on both sides. This frog shell is found under rocks and coral on reefs in shallow water, from North Carolina to Brazil.

CALIFORNIA FROG SHELL   1½–5 in.
This frog shell is a scavenger. Encircling rows of fine irregular threads sculpt the shell's surface. This edible mollusk is found in shallow water, from California to Baja California.

CHESTNUT FROG SHELL   1–2 in.
This frog shell is encircled with rows of fine beads. It is uncommon, and is found on rocks in moderately deep water, from southern Florida to the West Indies.

CORRUGATED FROG SHELL   2–3 in.
There is a double row of teeth on the outer lip. This shell is rare in southeastern Florida and the Caribbean, more common from lower (Baja) California to Ecuador.

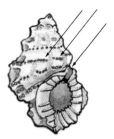

ST. THOMAS
FROG SHELL

CALIFORNIA
FROG SHELL

CHESTNUT
FROG SHELL

CORRUGATED
FROG SHELL

GASTROPODS: BUSYCON WHELKS

Whelk shells have a well-defined *siphonal canal* and a horny operculum. All whelks are carnivores or scavengers. The animal's head has a long, tubular extension called a proboscis, which has a mouth on the end. A whelk is an active predator that opens a clam or oyster shell by surrounding it with its muscular foot, which exerts a pulling force and opens the halves of the shell by suction. Then the whelk inserts its long proboscis to consume its prey.

Tiny whelk larvae (young) hatch from strings of egg capsules. The larvae have complete miniature shells and can crawl when they emerge.

KNOBBED WHELK   4–9 in.
Found in shallow water, from Massachusetts to Florida.

TURNIP WHELK   5–6 in.
Found in shallow water in the Gulf of Mexico.

LIGHTNING WHELK   3–5 in.
Although "right-handed" specimens have been found, this is considered a left-handed shell because it usually spirals to the left. It is found from North Carolina to Florida and westward to Texas.

PEAR WHELK   2½–5½ in.
Found from North Carolina to Mexico.

GASTROPODS: FIG SHELLS

Three of the 12 species in this family are found in the Caribbean region. Their shells are thin but strong and moderately large, with a very *short spire* on top.

COMMON FIG SHELL   2½–5 in.
Found in sand, from North Carolina to Mexico.

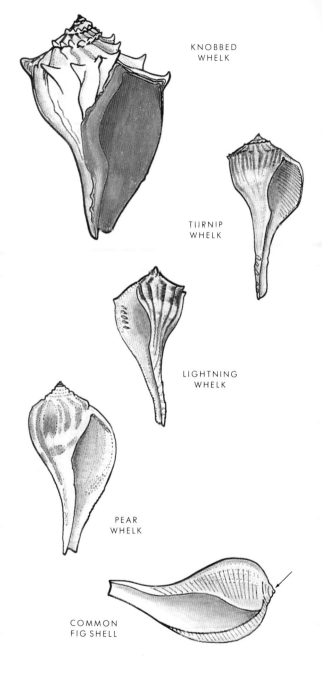

KNOBBED
WHELK

TURNIP
WHELK

LIGHTNING
WHELK

PEAR
WHELK

COMMON
FIG SHELL

GASTROPODS: MUREX SHELLS

Murex shells are abundant worldwide, in mostly tropical seas. Out of 700 species in the family, 400 are present in North America.

Murex shells have many shapes, but usually are thick and spiny. When the frondlike spines are coated with sea moss, the shell may be completely camouflaged amid rocks or on reefs. All murex shells have a horny operculum.

Murex snails are active carnivores. They use a rasplike muscular tongue called the radula to bore into the shells of clams or other bivalves and eat the animal inside. Murex snails produce fluids from a gland in the foot that aid in the boring action and may also anesthetize the prey. Some species have a long tooth at the base of the outer lip; this tooth is used, together with the suction of the foot, to pry open barnacles.

The sexes are separate.

SHORT-FROND MUREX   3–6 in.
(WEST INDIAN MUREX)

Found in deep water on oyster beds, from southern Florida to Brazil.

BEAU'S MUREX   3–4 in.

Uncommon. Found in deep water, from southern Florida to the West Indies.

FRILL-WING MUREX   1¾–2¾ in.

Found on rocks at the low-tide line, from Monterey, California, to Baja California. This murex is related to another murex called the Three-wing Murex, which is slightly larger and more triangular and is found from Catalina Island (off California) to central Baja California.

HEXAGONAL MUREX   1–1⅝ in.

Found under rocks on reefs, from the Florida Keys to the West Indies.

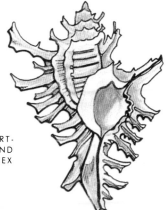

SHORT-
FROND
MUREX

BEAU'S
MUREX

FRILL-
WING
MUREX

HEXAGONAL
MUREX

GASTROPODS:
MUREX SHELLS AND RELATIVES

Murex shells and their relatives exude a yellowish fluid that smells like garlic. The juice from these animals is the basis of a world-famous dye that was first discovered by the greatest navigators of ancient times, the Phoenicians, who had many bases of trade and colonies in the Mediterranean. The Phoenicians had a monopoly in the production of cloth dyed with "royal Tyrian purple," a rare and brilliant color obtained solely from the living bodies of the murex snails. The emperors of Rome finally limited the use of this expensive color (the dye cost the equivalent of $10,000 a pound, and dyed wool cost $200 a pound), to their own garments. The principal city of the shell-dye industry was Tyre, which gave the dye its name.

To make the dye, the murex shells were broken and the animals were removed and placed in salt water for several days, then boiled and strained. When wool was dipped in the liquid, it turned a muddy purple. After it was set out to dry in the sun and then washed with soap and water or a weak lye solution, it became the gorgeous crimson color known as royal purple.

PINK-MOUTHED MUREX   3–6 in.
Found in moderately shallow water, from the Gulf of California to Peru.

CABRIT'S MUREX   1–3 in.
Found on sandy bottoms in shallow to deep water, from South Carolina to the West Indies.

CATALINA TROPHON   3–4 in.
Found in deep water off southern California.

MAUVE-MOUTHED DRILL   ¾–1¼ in.
Found on rocks from the low-tide line to deep water, from western Florida to the Florida Keys.

PINK-
MOUTHED
MUREX

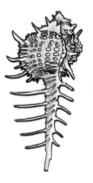

CABRIT'S
MUREX

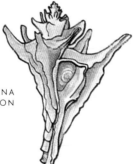

CATALINA
TROPHON

MAUVE-
MOUTHED
DRILL

GASTROPODS:
TRITONS AND RELATIVES

These shells are found in warm-temperate waters near coral reefs worldwide. They lay numerous horny egg capsules on rocks. The larvae (young) take several months to develop into adults and drift for long distances, which accounts for their wide distribution.

Most tritons grow a hairy periostracum (outer covering) that protects the shell. The shell has teeth around the aperture and a large horny operculum. Distorsios, which also belong to this group, have many fierce-looking teeth and a smaller operculum.

Tritons feed on other mollusks (both snails and clams) and on starfishes. First they secrete a paralyzing fluid that renders their prey helpless, then they insert their mouth part into the shell and eat the soft parts of the animal within.

The larger triton shells have been used as trumpets in many parts of the world since ancient times. After a small hole is drilled in the spire, the shell produces a trumpetlike sound when blown. The first nuclear submarine to sail completely around the world submerged in 1960 was named Triton, after the Greek sea god. For thousands of years, statues and pictures have shown the gods Triton and Neptune blowing triton-shell trumpets.

ATLANTIC TRUMPET   10—18 in.
(TRITON'S TRUMPET)
Found in moderately shallow water on reefs, from southern Florida to the West Indies.

GOLD-MOUTHED TRITON   2—3 in.
Found on reefs in shallow water, from southern Florida to the West Indies.

ATLANTIC DISTORSIO   ¾—3½ in.
Found on coarse sand among coral and rocks, from North Carolina to Brazil.

ATLANTIC
TRUMPET

GOLD-
MOUTHED
TRITON

ATLANTIC
DISTORSIO

GASTROPODS: VOLUTE SHELLS

A large family of elegant, spindle-shaped shells, found worldwide in warm deep water. Of about 200 species, 20 live in our range. The *columella*, or main pillar (the axis of the shell), has one or more *spiral ridges*. Volute shells are smooth, thick, and shiny. Most species do not have an operculum. These graceful, highly collectible shells come in a variety of beautiful patterns and colors.

Volutes are carnivorous. They eat small mollusks and other small marine animals.

MUSIC VOLUTE   2–2½ in.
One of the few volutes that has an operculum. The lines and "notes" that mark this shell appear to be lines of written music. This volute is found from the West Indies to South America.

DUBIOUS VOLUTE   To 2 in.
A slender, colorful shell; like the Dohrn's Volute (below), but with fewer spots. Rare; found in southern Florida and the Gulf of Mexico.

DOHRN'S VOLUTE   2–3 in.
Like the Junonia (next species), but lighter and more slender. A rare shell, found in southern Florida and the Gulf of Mexico.

JUNONIA (JUNO'S VOLUTE)   3–6 in.
When the snail inside is alive, the shell is covered with a thin periostracum. This volute is found from South Carolina to the Gulf of Mexico.

JOHNSTONE'S JUNONIA   3–6 in.
Shell covered with a thin periostracum. This volute is closely related to the Junonia, but has more vivid colors. It is found off the Florida Keys.

FLORIDA VOLUTE   3–4 in.
Found off the Florida Keys.

MUSIC
VOLUTE

DUBIOUS
VOLUTE

DOHRN'S
VOLUTE

JUNONIA
(JUNO'S VOLUTE)

JOHNSTONE'S
JUNONIA

FLORIDA
VOLUTE

GASTROPODS: TULIP SHELLS

These shells are also called band or spindle shells. Of about 200 species, 35 or so are found in warm-temperate waters off North America.

Tulip shells are smooth and thick. They have a graceful spindle shape with an elevated, sharply pointed spire and a somewhat curved, well-developed *siphonal canal*. There is a large, brown, horny operculum.

Tulip snails are aggressive predators. Slow and deliberate in movement, they feed on other mollusks. Tulip snails are found on coral reefs as well as on seaweed or sand, in shallow to deep water. The giant Florida Horse Conch is the largest single-shelled mollusk in North American seas.

FLORIDA HORSE CONCH   12–24 in.
(GIANT BANDED SHELL)
This is one of the largest gastropods found anywhere in the world. The shell is covered with a thick periostracum. It is found from North Carolina to Florida and the Gulf of Mexico.

TRUE TULIP SHELL   4–6 in.
There are *spiral folds* on the *columella*. Colors vary. Found from North Carolina to Florida and the Gulf of Mexico.

FLORIDA BANDED TULIP SHELL   2–4 in.
This shell is smaller and broader and has a shorter siphonal canal than the Banded Tulip (below). It is found from North Carolina to Florida and Alabama.

BANDED TULIP SHELL   2¼–4⅛ in.
Usually slightly larger than the Florida Banded Tulip Shell. This shell is found from Florida to Louisiana and Texas and south to Mexico.

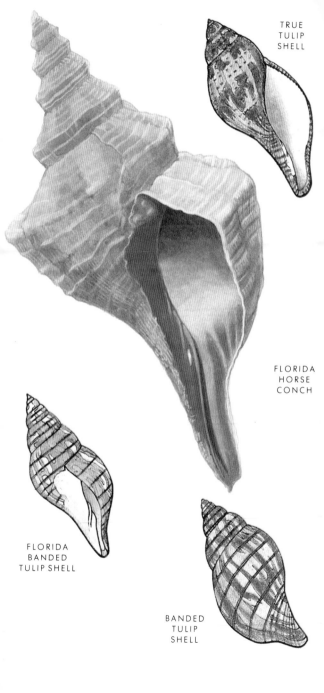

TRUE
TULIP
SHELL

FLORIDA
HORSE
CONCH

FLORIDA
BANDED
TULIP SHELL

BANDED
TULIP
SHELL

GASTROPODS: MITER SHELLS

Several hundred species of miters exist, but only a dozen or more live in North American waters. Miter snails live mainly in the shallow areas of our warm seas.

These spindle-shaped shells are thick and solid, with a sharp spire. Miters are often brightly colored. They are usually beaded or ribbed, but may also be smooth. The shell has a *siphonal notch* and prominent *spiral ridges on the columella.*

During the daytime miters stay hidden under rocks or coral rubble. At night they burrow in sand, but extend their long, retractable snout out of the sand to feed on clams and marine worms. Some miters have a venom gland, which is used to paralyze their prey, and give off a smelly purple fluid when disturbed. These snails are scavengers as well as carnivores.

These small, slender jewels are very popular with collectors. The best time to find miters is at the turn of the tide, when there is a low tide at night.

ROYAL FLORIDA MITER   1½–2 in.
This rare shell is found from southern Florida to the West Indies.

IDA'S MITER   To 2½ in.
Found in southern California.

HENDERSON'S MITER   To ¼ in.
This tiny shell is found from southeastern Florida to the Caribbean.

BARBADOS MITER   1–1¾ in.
Found from southeastern Florida to Brazil.

SULCATE MITER   To 1 in.
Found from North Carolina to the West Indies.

ROYAL
FLORIDA
MITER

IDA'S
MITER

HENDERSON'S
MITER

BARBADOS
MITER

SULCATE
MITER

GASTROPODS: SPINDLE SHELLS

There are more than 50 species of spindle shells, found in tropical waters all over the world. These spindle-shaped shells may be large and heavy, but they are also graceful. They have a long, many-whorled spire that tapers to a point. The *columella* is *smooth*, with no circular ridges, and the outer lip is not thickened. The shell's surface is protected by a periostracum (skinlike covering). The *siphonal canal* is long, straight or slightly curved, and open. The dark brown, horny operculum completely seals the aperture, which is oval.

These snails are slow and deliberate. They feed on marine worms, barnacles, clams, and snails. Spindle shells are found in pairs, on sand, and on or underneath rocks and kelp.

SANTA BARBARA SPINDLE 2¼–5¼ in.
An uncommon shell, found on coarse sand or rocks in deep water, from Oregon to California.

ORNAMENTED SPINDLE To 3 in.
Found on sand in moderately deep water in the Gulf of Mexico.

COUÉ'S SPINDLE 2¼–4½ in.
This shell is named for the French ship's captain who discovered it around 1855. An uncommon shell, found on sand in deep water in the Gulf of Mexico.

PAINTED SPINDLE ½–1 in.
Found on or under rocks and kelp in moderately deep water, from Monterey, California, to Baja California.

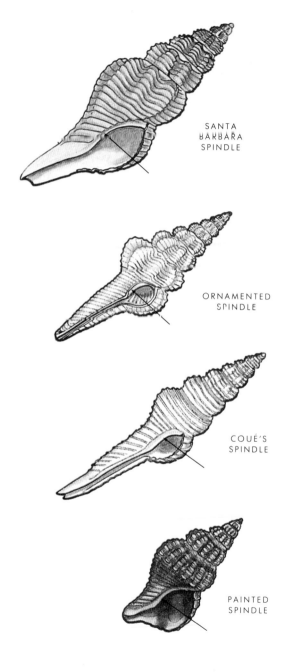

SANTA
BARBARA
SPINDLE

ORNAMENTED
SPINDLE

COUÉ'S
SPINDLE

PAINTED
SPINDLE

GASTROPODS: TURRID SHELLS

This is the largest family of mollusks, with about 1500 species found all over the world. Four hundred species live along both our coasts, in water ranging from low-tide level to 10,000 ft. deep. This ancient group of shells evolved over 100 million years ago.

The shape of these shells varies widely, from regally graceful to dull and squat. The conical spire, which is sometimes shaped like a turret, is widely variable: it may be greatly elongate or broad. The siphonal canal may be short or long and slender. All turrid shells have a characteristic notch called the *turrid notch*. This notch is found in the upper part of the outer lip. A horny operculum may or may not be present.

All turrids can secrete a stupefying venom that renders their prey senseless. This poison, used together with the radula — a feeding organ — is the way the mollusk feeds and protects itself. In some species the radula is armed with harpoon-shaped teeth; in others the teeth are in several rows (see p. 7).

WHITE GIANT TURRID   2½–5 in.
Found in sand in deep water, from North Carolina to Florida to the West Indies.

OYSTER TURRID   ½–1 in.
Found in sand and rubble in shallow to deep water, from North Carolina to the Virgin Islands.

PERVERSE TURRID   1½–2 in.
This shell is among the few cold-water species that are "left-handed"—the shell spirals to the left as the animal grows. This turrid is found from Alaska to southern California.

CARPENTER'S TURRID   1¾–3¾ in.
Found on mud in deep water, from central to Baja Califonia.

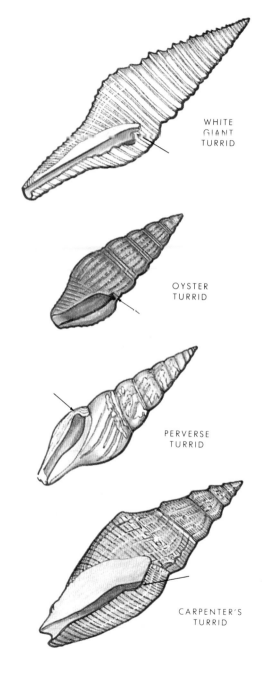

WHITE
GIANT
TURRID

OYSTER
TURRID

PERVERSE
TURRID

CARPENTER'S
TURRID

GASTROPODS: CONE SHELLS

There are 400 to 500 species of these beautiful, solid shells living in tropical and subtropical seas. About 30 species live in our area.

Cones may be tiny to huge, short to long, and slim to broad. The top of the shell can vary from flat to rounded or sharply pointed and everything in between, and the shoulders may be sloped, rounded, or squared. Most cone snails have colorful shells—some are striking, with brilliant colors, but others are plain and dull colored. The shell surface can be smooth, knobbed, grooved, or corded. Within each species, the color and pattern of each individual shell may vary considerably. Even though their size, shape, and surface textures vary, all cone shells have one thing in common: they are most distinctly *cone-shaped.*

Cone snails produce a venomous poison from a gland within their bodies. The poison gland is connected with the harpoon-like teeth on the radula. Although no deadly species occur in our area, all cone snails should be handled with extreme caution.

See also p. 40.

GLORY-OF-THE-ATLANTIC CONE　　1–1¾ in.
An uncommon shell with a rosy aperture. Found in moderately deep water, from southern Florida to the West Indies.

CROWN CONE　　　　　　　　　　1½–3 in.
Found on reefs, from southern Florida to Brazil.

JASPER CONE　　　　　　　　　　½–1 in.
Found in shallow water, from southern Florida to Brazil.

MAZE'S CONE　　　　　　　　　　1½–2 in.
Found in deep water, from the Florida Keys to Brazil.

ATLANTIC ALPHABET CONE　　　1¾–3 in.
Found in shallow water, from Florida to Mexico.

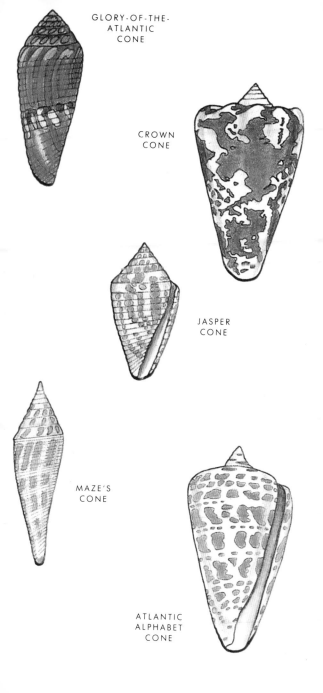

GLORY-OF-THE-ATLANTIC CONE

CROWN CONE

JASPER CONE

MAZE'S CONE

ATLANTIC ALPHABET CONE

GASTROPODS:
CONE SHELLS, *continued*

CARROT CONE   1–2 in.
The interior of the aperture is pinkish. The shell is usually a solid color; rare specimens have a lighter band around the middle. This cone is found in moderately deep water (at depths below 15 ft.), from Florida to the West Indies.

CALIFORNIA CONE   ¾–1½ in.
Live snails have a thick, reddish brown, velvetlike periostracum covering the grayish white shell. This cone is found in shallow water, from California to Baja California.

FLORIDA CONE   1–2 in.
Live snails have a thin brown periostracum covering the shell. This cone is found in sand in shallow to deep water (up to 90 ft. deep), from North Carolina to Florida.

SOZON'S CONE   2–4 in.
This cone may be smooth or marked with *spiral threads* at the lower end of the shell. It has 2 characteristic *whitish bands* around the middle. Large specimens are collector's items. Sozon's Cone is found in deep water, from South Carolina to the Gulf of Mexico.

GOLDEN-BANDED CONE   2–3 in.
Several *light yellow bands* encircle the shell. This cone is uncommon to rare. It is found in moderately deep water, from the Florida Keys to Yucatan, Mexico.

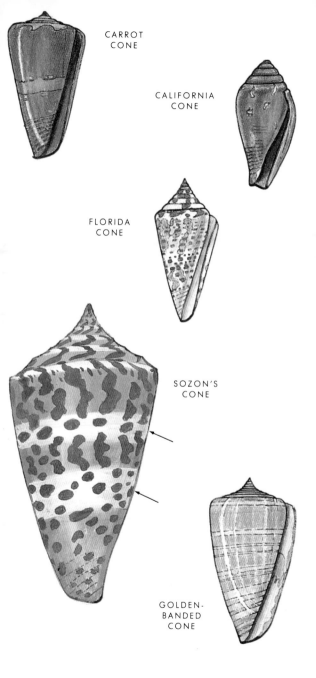

CARROT
CONE

CALIFORNIA
CONE

FLORIDA
CONE

SOZON'S
CONE

GOLDEN-
BANDED
CONE

GASTROPODS: DOVE SHELLS

This family of small, charming, mostly tropical or semitropical snails consists of several hundred species, with around 76 living in our range. These shells are usually shiny but vary in size, shape, and ornamentation: doves may be smooth or sculptured, ovate (egg-shaped) to elongate. The spire may be high or low, sharply pointed or broad. Color patterns can be striking, but vary from one shell to the next of the same species. All dove shells have an operculum.

The family is divided into 2 subfamilies: one group is mostly herbivorous and feeds on algae (seaweed); the other is mostly carnivorous and feeds on other mollusks as well as detritus (minute particles of marine life) and algae. Doves live on rocks, in sand, or on coral, in shallow or deep water.

WHITE-SPOTTED DOVE SHELL   ⅜–½ in.
A carnivorous dove. Colors are various shades of brown; spots may be large or small. This dove is found from southeastern Florida to northern Brazil.

SMOOTH DOVE SHELL   ½–¾ in.
Found under stones on sand in the intertidal zone, from the Florida Keys to the West Indies.

CARINATE DOVE SHELL   ¼–⅜ in.
A *strongly toothed* shell. Found on seagrass, from southern Alaska to Mexico.

WELL-RIBBED DOVE SHELL   ⅜–½ in.
This shell resembles the Greedy Dove Shell (below), but is taller and has a more slender spire, and a *beaded suture line.* A carnivorous mollusk, found from Massachusetts to Florida.

GREEDY DOVE SHELL   ⅜–¾ in.
Found among seagrass, from Massachusetts to Florida.

WHITE-
SPOTTED
DOVE SHELL

SMOOTH
DOVE
SHELL

CARINATE
DOVE
SHELL

WELL-RIBBED
DOVE SHELL

GREEDY
DOVE
SHELL

GASTROPODS: AUGERS

Augers are most attractive collectibles. Of the 150 or so species in this family, 20 live in North American seas. They range from a tiny, ½-in. long shell to a large, 8⅞-in. long shell.

All augers are tall and pointed, elongate, and narrow, with many whorls or turns. There is a *short siphonal canal.* The outer lip is sharp and the base of the inner lip is twisted. The aperture is small. The operculum is thin, horny, and shaped like a comma — round on one end and curving to a point on the other. No periostracum covers the shell; when you see an auger shell with a live snail inside, it is smooth and shiny.

Some auger snails have barbed radular teeth and a gland that secretes a mild poison, but there are no dangerous species in American waters. These mollusks feed on marine worms and live just below the surface in sandy mud or coral sand, in shallow tropical or subtropical waters.

FLAME AUGER　　　　　　　　3¾–6¼ in.
Our largest auger shell. Found from southeastern Florida to the West Indies.

GRAY ATLANTIC AUGER　　　　1–2 in.
This shell has a velvety look when wet. It is found from southeastern Florida to Brazil.

SALLÉ'S AUGER　　　　　　　½–1½ in.
Found from North Carolina to Texas.

SHINY ATLANTIC AUGER　　　1–2 in.
Found from southeastern Florida to the West Indies.

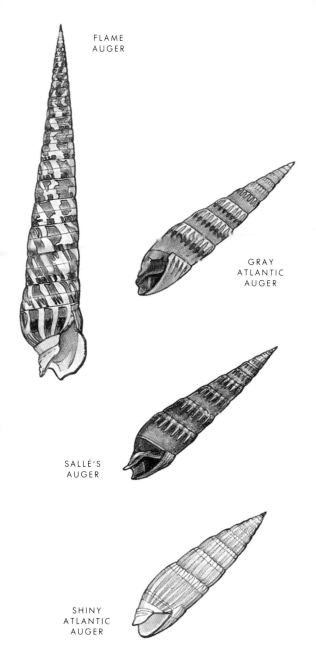

FLAME
AUGER

GRAY
ATLANTIC
AUGER

SALLÉ'S
AUGER

SHINY
ATLANTIC
AUGER

GASTROPODS: WENTLETRAPS

A large family of hundreds of species of small, fragile, white, or slightly tinted shells, found worldwide in all seas.

These loosely coiled, spiral sculptures are called wentletraps, a Dutch word meaning "winding staircase." These "staircase shells" are delicately graceful in shape, which makes them a favorite of shell collectors. On each pointed, conical shell are a series of raised ribs called *varices*, which record pauses in the shell's growth: each one was the shell's outer lip at an earlier stage. The round aperture of the shell is protected by a horny operculum.

Wentletrap snails are carnivores — they feed on small sea anemones, tearing off big pieces with their many rows of file-like radular teeth. The pinkish purple dye the wentletraps secrete is thought to have an anesthetic effect, which helps subdue their prey.

BLADED WENTLETRAP ⅜–⅞ in.
Found in shallow water, from southern Florida to Argentina.

LAMELLOSE WENTLETRAP ⅝–1¼ in.
Light reddish brown markings distinguish this wentletrap. It is found in shallow water, from southern Florida to western Africa.

KREBS' WENTLETRAP ½–⅞ in.
Found in coral sand, from South Carolina to Brazil.

ANGULATE WENTLETRAP ½–⅞ in.
One of the most common wentletraps. It is found in shallow water in sand or rubble, from New York to Florida and west to Texas.

SCALLOP-EDGED WENTLETRAP ⅜–¾ in.
(SCULPTURED WENTLETRAP)
Found on rocks at the low-tide line, from southern California to Panama.

BLADED
WENTLETRAP

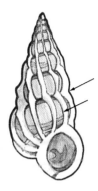

LAMELLOSE
WENTLETRAP

KREBS'
WENTLETRAP

ANGULATE
WENTLETRAP

SCALLOP-EDGED
WENTLETRAP

GASTROPODS: TOP SHELLS

A large family, with 180 species living in our waters.

Tops vary widely in size, height, and width, but they are all spirals with a conical or pyramidal shape. The surface varies in texture and luster: some tops are smooth, others are sculptured; some are shiny, others dull. Top shells are made mostly of mother-of-pearl. In some jewel-quality top shells the pearly luster is hidden by a dull, thin, shelly layer. All have a lovely iridescent interior and a thin, horny operculum.

Female top snails are larger than males. These herbivorous snails feed on algae (seaweed) and plant detritus. If you happen to see a rock covered with seaweed or other growth with rounded knobs or projections that are similarly coated and seem to move, it very well may be that these are feeding top shells that are perfectly camouflaged. They are found in seaweed, on sand, gravel, or rocks, in warm or cold seas throughout the world. On a sunny day, you can find tops clinging to kelp fronds.

NORRIS TOP SHELL 1¼–2¼ in.
Found in shallow water, from California to Baja California.

SUPERB GAZA SHELL 1⅜–1½ in.
This iridescent top shell is found in deep water, from the West Indies to the Gulf of California.

WEST INDIAN TOP SHELL (MAGPIE) 2–4½ in.
This snail is eaten in chowder. It can be found between the high- and low-tide line in the West Indies.

PACIFIC RINGED TOP SHELL ⅝–1¼ in.
Found in the intertidal zone, from southern Alaska to northern Baja California.

SAY'S TOP SHELL ⅝–1¼ in.
Found in deep water, from North Carolina to Florida.

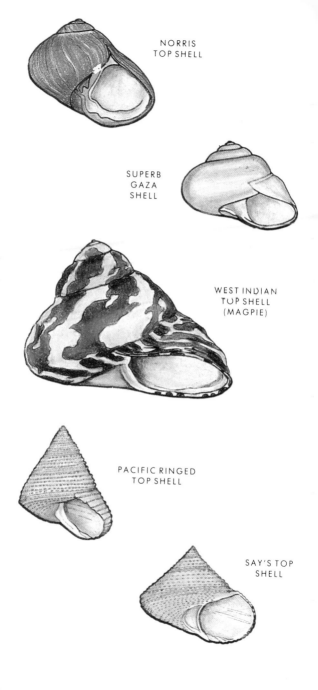

NORRIS
TOP SHELL

SUPERB
GAZA
SHELL

WEST INDIAN
TOP SHELL
(MAGPIE)

PACIFIC RINGED
TOP SHELL

SAY'S TOP
SHELL

GASTROPODS: TEGULA SHELLS

Tegula shells are members of the top shell family (see p. 48). Out of several hundred species worldwide, there are over a dozen tegulas in North American waters. Most of them live among rocks on the coast of California; only a few live on the Atlantic coast of Florida.

Tegula shells are coiled, conical, sturdy, and thick. A hollow called the *umbilicus* is visible on the flattened underside of the shell. A thin layer of dark shelly material covers the shell. When this outer layer is worn or scraped off, a lovely iridescent, nacreous shell surface is revealed. The interior of the shell is also made of nacre, or mother-of-pearl.

All tegulas are herbivores, meaning they are plant-eating snails. The largest specimens of each species are found in the warmest waters within the range where the species lives.

BROWN TEGULA   ¾–2 in.
Shells of living snails are often covered with algae (seaweed). This tegula is found among rocks at low tide, from Oregon to the Santa Barbara Islands, California.

QUEEN TEGULA   ¾–2 in.
This shell is covered with a dark, purple-brown layer. The base of the shell is concave. The interior is a pearly gold. This tegula is eagerly sought by collectors. It is found in deep water, from Catalina Island to the Gulf of California.

SPECKLED TEGULA   ¾–1⅝ in.
Found on rocks intertidally — between the high- and low-tide lines — from San Francisco to Baja California.

GILDED TEGULA   ⅛–1 in.
The thin outer layer on this shell is dark gray to black. This tegula is found among rocks close to shore, from southern California to Mexico.

BROWN
TEGULA

QUEEN
TEGULA

SPECKLED
TEGULA

GILDED
TEGULA

GASTROPODS: NERITES

A large family of several hundred species, with 13 species in our waters. Nerites are mostly round, with a *low spire* that can look like just a swirl on top of the shell. They may be smooth or sculptured. The *aperture* is *semicircular* and may be toothed or smooth on the edge. The shelly operculum has a small, armlike projection on its inner side. The variety of patterns and colors on most of these charming little jewels is infinite. They are always interesting.

Nerites feed on algae (seaweed) and live in large colonies on rocks and eelgrass near coral reefs; a few species even live on dry land and in trees in swampy areas. These snails live in salty water, such as bays or tidepools; brackish water, such as marshes or inland waterways; and fresh water, such as springs. Some nerites have the ability to store water in their shells by sealing the aperture with the operculum. This helps keep them from drying out when they are beyond the water's edge or are exposed by low tides.

ZEBRA NERITE ⅜–½ in.
Found on intertidal rocks, from eastern Florida to the Caribbean.

EMERALD NERITE To ¼ in.
Found on eelgrass, from Bermuda to Florida and south to Brazil.

VIRGIN NERITE ¼–¾ in.
Found on brackish mud flats, from Bermuda to Florida and south to Brazil.

POLISHED NERITE To ½ in.
Found in shallow water along Hawaiian shores.

BLEEDING-TOOTH NERITE ¾–1½ in.
Found on intertidal rocks, from southeastern Florida to Brazil. This nerite is named for the *reddish stain* around the *prominent teeth* at the edge of the aperture.

ZEBRA
NERITE

EMERALD
NERITE

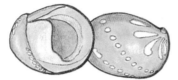

VIRGIN
NERITE

POLISHED
NERITE

BLEEDING-
TOOTH
NERITE

GASTROPODS: JANTHINAS

Janthinas, also called purple snails or violet snails, are thin, fragile-shelled snails. They are pelagic, a word meaning "floating in the open seas." Janthinas are found floating together in huge colonies in the warm-temperate seas off both coasts of the U.S. They cannot survive in cold water. Since these beautiful snails are Gulf Stream travelers, rafts of hundreds of them are blown ashore not only in Florida, but as far north as Massachusetts. Each animal produces lavender, *jelly-like bubbles* of mucus and cements them to its foot, which allows the snail to float. Some janthinas attach their eggs to the underside of the bubble raft.

Janthinas are camouflaged by their color, which keeps them relatively safe from predators. Tinted with various shades of purple, usually lighter above and a deeper violet below, janthinas blend with the sea when seen by birds from above, and merge with the sky when seen by fish from below.

A janthina shell consists of several whorls and is globular (rounded) or angled and somewhat conical. The shell has a slightly elevated spire. The aperture is large and elongate, with no operculum. When irritated the snail exudes a purple fluid.

Janthinas feed on jellyfish and are usually found among them; they also eat other animals they come upon in the open sea.

COMMON JANTHINA   1–2½ in.
This janthina is a lighter shade of purple above.

GLOBE JANTHINA   ¼–1 in.
This rounded but elongate shell is evenly shaded.

PALLID JANTHINA   ¼–1½ in.
The bottom of the aperture is beautifully rounded. It is a whitened pinkish violet.

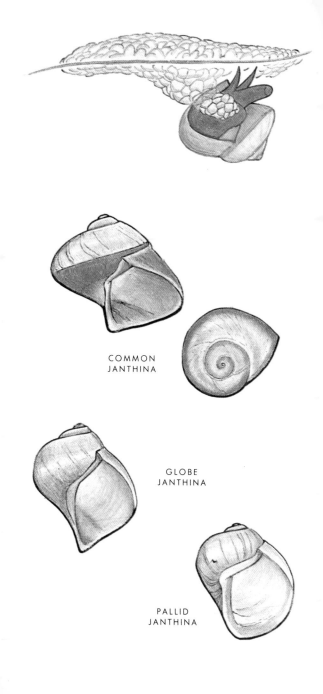

COMMON
JANTHINA

GLOBE
JANTHINA

PALLID
JANTHINA

GASTROPODS: COWRIES

A large family of about 190 species, found in all the warm seas. Six species are found in the Caribbean region and 5 off the warm coasts of the U.S., including one in California. Cowries live under rocks and feed on algae (seaweed) at night.

Cowries are very shiny, brilliantly colored shells, rounded to oval, with a long aperture that is *toothed* on both lips. The shell appears to be an empty chamber with an aperture but no spire, whorls, or other features. Not true! If you cut the shell in half crosswise you will find all of these things inside the shell.

A cowry is a typical univalve (single-shelled snail). As in other univalves, the fleshy mantle produces lime to make the shell. The cowry's mantle is large — when extended, it usually covers the entire shell. It also produces the material that makes the outer surface of the shell so incredibly smooth and polished.

These glossy, jewel-like shells have been used in art, for trade, money, jewelry, and religious symbols since the time of early man.

ATLANTIC YELLOW COWRY   ½–1¼ in.
Top whitish, speckled with orange-brown. This cowry is found from North Carolina to Brazil.

ATLANTIC GRAY COWRY   ¾–1 in.
Found from North Carolina to Brazil.

MEASLED COWRY   2–4 in.
Base tan. Found from North Carolina to Brazil.

CHESTNUT COWRY   1–2½ in.
Base pure white. Found from central California to Baja California.

DEER COWRY   3½–5 in.
This cowry has brown teeth around the aperture. Found from southern Florida to the West Indies.

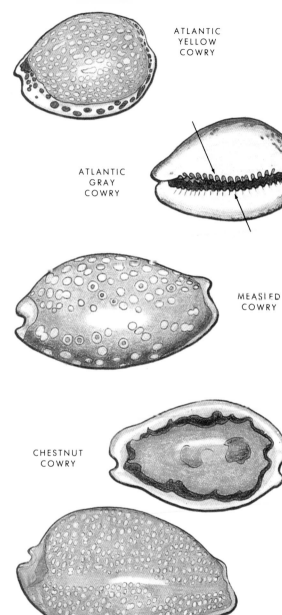

ATLANTIC
YELLOW
COWRY

ATLANTIC
GRAY
COWRY

MEASLED
COWRY

CHESTNUT
COWRY

DEER
COWRY

GASTROPODS: MARGINELLAS

Marginellas are tiny, brightly colored shells that appear enameled. There are about 300 species worldwide, in temperate and tropical seas. Marginellas are carnivores; they live among algae (seaweed) under stones.

Marginellas vary in shape from ovate (egg-shaped) to almost round. The spire is short to flat. The outer lip of the shell is finely toothed or smooth, and has a *thickened margin* that gives the family its name. The aperture of the shell is long and narrow. There are slanting ridges on the columella. No operculum is present. A fleshy mantle covers the shell while the snail is in motion, traveling effortlessly and swiftly over the bottom. Marginellas can disappear quickly in the sand.

Indians living along the eastern coast of the U.S. caught marginellas by baiting their fishing lines with oysters. Marginella shells are one of the types of shells used for shell money called "roanoke." The tips of the shells were filed off and the shells were strung. Marginellas were so plentiful that they were valuable only to inland Indians, far from the sea.

CARMINE MARGINELLA   To ⅓ in.
Found from southern Florida to the West Indies.

TAN MARGINELLA   To ⅓ in.
Found from North Carolina to the Caribbean.

ORANGE MARGINELLA   To ¾ in.
Found from southern Florida to the West Indies.

ORANGE-BANDED MARGINELLA   To ½ in.
Found from North Carolina to the Caribbean.

PRINCESS MARGINELLA   To ½ in.
Found from the Florida Keys to the West Indies.

CARMINE
MARGINELLA

ORANGE
MARGINELLA

TAN
MARGINELLA

ORANGE-
BANDED
MARGINELLA

PRINCESS
MARGINELLA

GASTROPODS: OLIVE SHELLS

Olive shells are a large family of 300 species. They are found in shallow water on sandy sea bottoms, on both coasts of the U.S. and in all tropical seas.

Olive shells have been used since prehistoric times for jewelry and ornamentation. They are shaped like a pointed olive. The aperture is long and narrow; there is no operculum. The columella is marked with fine lines and ridges.

Olive shells are small, but the animals that live in them are relatively large. When extended, the snail's mantle may cover the entire shell, keeping it smooth and shiny. Microscopic tubes in the mantle secrete a dye that makes the patterns on each shell. Each snail has its own pattern; each individual has slight variations in color and design that distinguish it from others of its own kind, for its entire life.

Olive snails eat worms, bivalves (see p. 78), and crabs. An olive snail uses its large foot to grab its prey and pull it down into the sand to feed on it.

PURPLE DWARF OLIVE $\frac{1}{2}-1\frac{1}{2}$ in.
Found from British Columbia to Baja California.

WEST INDIAN DWARF OLIVE $\frac{1}{2}-1\frac{1}{4}$ in.
Found from Florida to Texas and south to the West Indies.

JASPER DWARF OLIVE $\frac{1}{2}-\frac{7}{8}$ in.
Found from southeastern Florida to Venezuela.

NETTED OLIVE $1\frac{1}{8}-2\frac{1}{4}$ in.
Found from southeastern Florida to Venezuela.

LETTERED OLIVE $1\frac{3}{4}-2\frac{3}{4}$ in.
Found from North Carolina to Texas and south to Brazil.

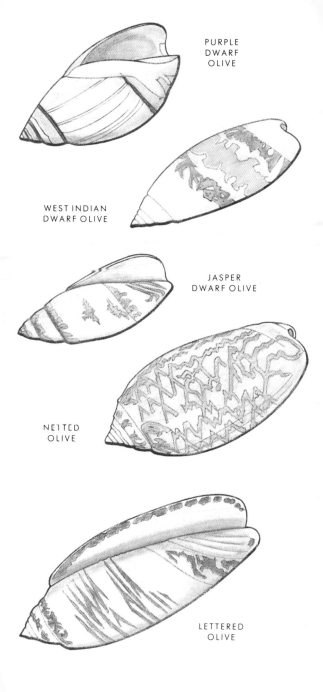

PURPLE
DWARF
OLIVE

WEST INDIAN
DWARF OLIVE

JASPER
DWARF OLIVE

NETTED
OLIVE

LETTERED
OLIVE

GASTROPODS: BUBBLE SHELLS

Bubble shells are found worldwide and on both coasts of the U.S., in warm and tropical seas. Bubbles burrow in sand in shallow water and crawl out at night to feed on algae and prey on other mollusks at low tide.

The form of these smooth shells is a symphony of simplicity. The shell's long aperture is surrounded by a frail, flaring outer lip that sweeps down from the top of the body whorl to far below the bottom of the aperture, where it widens to make the overall line a lovely oblong, oval, or rounded shape. The shell is often smaller than the animal that lives inside it. When extended, the mantle does not completely cover the shell.

Each bubble snail has 2 pairs of feelers and has both male and female sex organs.

GREEN PAPER BUBBLE $\frac{1}{2}-\frac{3}{4}$ in.
Found from Puget Sound to the Gulf of California.

COMMON ATLANTIC BUBBLE $\frac{1}{2}-1\frac{1}{8}$ in.
Found from Florida to Brazil.

CALIFORNIA BUBBLE $1\frac{1}{2}-2\frac{1}{2}$ in.
(GOULD'S BUBBLE)
Found from southern California to the Gulf of California.

LINED BUBBLE $\frac{3}{4}-1\frac{3}{4}$ in.
Found from southern Florida to Brazil.

PINK BUBBLE To 1 in.
Found on Hawaiian shores.

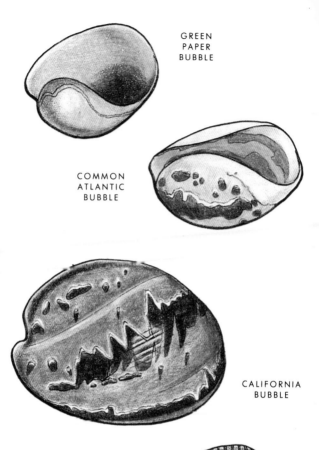

GREEN
PAPER
BUBBLE

COMMON
ATLANTIC
BUBBLE

CALIFORNIA
BUBBLE

LINED
BUBBLE

PINK
BUBBLE

GASTROPODS: TRUE LIMPETS

True limpets are found worldwide. There are around 35 species and subspecies in North America. A limpet shell is conical or cap-shaped, without spiral whorls. Limpets that live in rough shallow water generally have lower shells than those that live in deep calm water. Unlike keyhole limpets (see p. 66), true limpets have no hole in the top of the shell, just an opening at the base.

Limpets creep on rocks or seaweed at night. They munch on bits of algae, scraping them off with the rows of sharp teeth on the radula. There is a gill above the snail's head or a fold in the mantle's edge that functions as gills.

The interior of a limpet shell is smooth and glossy, iridescent or porcelain-like. The muscle scar is U-shaped, and the muscle is able to grip rocks like a strong, horseshoe-shaped magnet. You could lift a rock weighing several pounds with a limpet. The only way to remove a limpet is by slipping a knife under it and lifting up.

Limpets may be eaten and the shells are sometimes used as jewelry.

WHITE-CAP LIMPET   ¾–1¾ in.
Interior iridescent. Found from Alaska to Baja California.

ATLANTIC PLATE LIMPET   ⅞–1¾ in.
Interior bluish white, with a brown center and brown markings on the edge. Found in arctic seas off Alaska and south to New York.

GIANT OWL LIMPET   1¾–4¼ in.
Exterior brown, with white spots that are usually covered with algae. The muscle scar is somewhat owl-shaped. This limpet is found from Washington to Baja California.

ROUGH LIMPET   ¾–2 in.
Interior gray, with a dark green center and brown spots on the edge. Found from Alaska to Mexico.

WHITE-CAP
LIMPET

ATLANTIC
PLATE
LIMPET

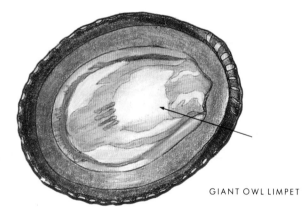

GIANT OWL LIMPET

ROUGH
LIMPET

GASTROPODS: KEYHOLE LIMPETS

Keyhole limpets live in low intertidal zones in warm-temperate seas worldwide. There are 100 or so species in North America on both coasts.

Keyhole limpets vary in size from tiny to huge. Their shapes range from round to oval to shieldlike. Each volcano-shaped shell has a *hole, slit, notch, or groove,* usually at or near its top. The hole may be round, oval, elongate, or keyhole-like. Some species have only a slit at the front end of the shell. The outer surface of the shell may be strongly ribbed or sculptured, and the inner surface is porcelain-like, with a horseshoe-shaped muscle scar.

When the tide is in, water is drawn in through the underside of the shell and washes over the limpet's 2 sets of well-developed gill plumes, providing the snail with oxygen. The water then carries away the snail's wastes through the outlet hole ("keyhole").

Keyhole limpets are mainly vegetarians. They cling to coral and rocks with their broad foot and scrape off algae with the rows of fine teeth on their radula. Keyhole limpets are usually covered with sea moss, which helps camouflage them on rocks.

We can eat these mollusks and they are used for ornamentation.

ROUGH KEYHOLE LIMPET   1–2¾ in.
Interior white. Found from Alaska to Baja California.

CANCELLATED FLESHY LIMPET   ⅝–1½ in.
The shell interior has faint pastel rays. Found from Florida to Brazil.

VOLCANO LIMPET   1–1⅝ in.
Interior white. Found from Florida Keys to the West Indies.

LINNÉ'S PUNCTURELLA   ¼–½ in.
Interior white, with a tiny, funnel-shaped cup bordering the slit. Found from Alaska to Baja California.

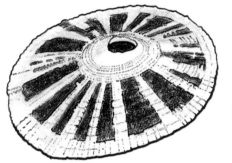

ROUGH
KEYHOLE
LIMPET

CANCELLATED
FLESHY
LIMPET

VOLCANO
LIMPET

LINNÉ'S
PUNCTURELLA

GASTROPODS: ABALONES

Abalones are among the best-known shells of California. Of about 100 species worldwide, 10 reside on our Pacific Coast and one tiny deep-water species lives in the Florida Straits.

These shells are very decorative, with an iridescent layer of mother-of-pearl inside. They have been used for adornment since early times. Abalones are also very popular as food and are now protected by law from commercial overfishing. These laws are a good example of conservation laws that work, for if abalones had not been protected, they might have become extinct by now.

The exterior of an abalone shell can be smooth or textured. A small, low spire consisting of a few whorls is evident at one end of the last whorl. The last whorl of the shell is usually oval and saucerlike; it has a row of holes that are located directly over the abalone's gills. Water enters through the aperture, or large opening, underneath the edge of the last whorl. The water washes over the gills, bringing oxygen, then leaves through the row of holes, taking away wastes. As each new hole is formed, the last is sealed from within the shell.

Abalones live on rocks near or below the water line, often in cracks and crevices. An abalone protects itself by letting the rock on which it lives act as its operculum. It can clamp itself down tightly and can withstand violent wave action. At night abalones creep about on a large muscular foot to forage for algae, always returning to their home spot at dawn.

RED ABALONE   To 12 in.
The best-tasting abalone. Found mostly in water 20 to 40 ft. deep, from Oregon to Baja California.

GREEN ABALONE   6–8 in.
Beautiful as well as delicious. Found in water 10 to 25 ft. deep, from Oregon to Baja California.

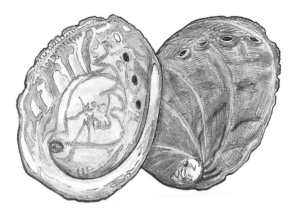

RED ABALONE

GREEN ABALONE

GASTROPODS:
CUP-AND-SAUCERS

Cup-and-saucer shells are found in both warm and cold seas worldwide, and on both coasts of the U.S. They resemble limpets (see p. 66) and are shaped like a little coiled cap, with a tiny droopy peak on top. Inside the shell, toward the peak, is a *shelly, cuplike projection* that helps support the animal's body and protect its soft parts.

These snails are filter feeders — they strain bits of algae and other microscopic plant life through their gills. Food enters the mantle cavity with the seawater that is drawn in. The food is trapped, covered by a secretion, and then drawn into the snail's stomach by the radula (file-like tongue).

Young cup-and-saucer shells can move about freely, but after 2 years they attach themselves to a rock or shell and remain there, rarely moving, for the rest of their life.

STRIATE CUP-AND-SAUCER   ½–1⅜ in.
Found in moderately deep to deep water, from southern California to Florida.

SPINY CUP-AND-SAUCER   ¾–2 in.
Found in water from a few feet to 180 feet deep, from California to Chile.

WEST INDIAN   ¾–1 in.
CUP-AND-SAUCER
Found in shallow water, from southern Florida to the West Indies.

STRIATE CUP-AND-SAUCER

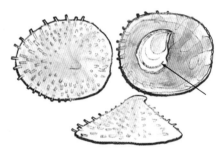

SPINY CUP-AND-SAUCER

WEST INDIAN
CUP-AND-SAUCER

GASTROPODS: SLIPPER SHELLS

Slipper shells are found in shallow water in both warm and cold seas all over the world, and on both coasts of the U.S. They are often called "boat shells." When you see one upside down, it looks like an old sailing ship with a flat rear deck. This *raised "deck"* sometimes covers almost half of the inside of the shell. This shelf supports the animal and protects its soft digestive parts.

Slipper shells are spiraled on the exterior and may be smooth or textured. The shape of the shell varies according to the object on which the snail lives, but it is mostly oval. The shell looks like a skier's hat without the tassel. The apex, or top, droops off to one side.

Like cup-and-saucer snails (see p. 70), these mollusks settle down after 2 years of drifting, and remain attached to the same rock or empty shell for the rest of their lives. They can move about slightly, but most of them do not.

Like cup-and-saucers, slipper snails possess both male and female sex organs. During spawning season the sexes alternate; males change into females and vice versa.

SPINY SLIPPER SHELL $\frac{1}{2}-1\frac{1}{4}$ in.
Found from all southern states to the West Indies, and from California to Chile.

SPOTTED SLIPPER SHELL $\frac{1}{2}-1\frac{1}{2}$ in.
Found in western Florida.

ATLANTIC SLIPPER SHELL $\frac{3}{4}-2\frac{1}{2}$ in.
Found from Canada to Florida and also on the West Coast.

CONVEX SLIPPER SHELL $\frac{3}{8}-\frac{3}{4}$ in.
Found from Massachusetts to the West Indies, and also along the Pacific Coast.

SPINY SLIPPER SHELL

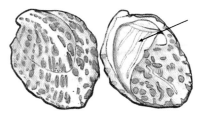

SPOTTED SLIPPER SHELL

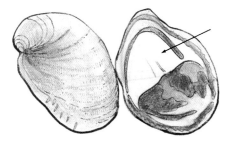

ATLANTIC SLIPPER SHELL

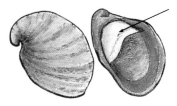

CONVEX SLIPPER SHELL

CHITONS

Chitons have been around for about 570 million years and are the most primitive mollusks. There are about 500 species worldwide. One hundred live on our Pacific Coast; fewer live on the Atlantic side.

Chitons are nicknamed "coat-of-mail" because they have *8 overlapping plates*, like medieval armor, on the back. These shingle-like plates are held together by a *leathery girdle* of muscular tissue, the mantle. The articulated shell lets the animal conform to various contours — it can draw itself up and tighten itself down on a rock. The plates may be smooth or sculptured with ridges or knobs. The girdle may have spikes, bristles, hair, scales, or granules, or it may be smooth. When dried and mounted, the girdle shows an assortment of colors, including shades of white, yellow, blue, pink, and orange.

Chitons live under or on rocks, in cracks, pockets, and on other hard surfaces such as empty shells and stones and are perfectly camouflaged to match their surroundings. At twilight, chitons creep out to dine on diatoms and other algae, or sometimes even on small animals. At dawn each chiton returns to its home spot. Chitons cling tenaciously to rocks in intertidal zones and live in deep water as well as in tidepools in shallow water. You would have to slip a knife blade under a chiton to dislodge it from its rock. A chiton can curl up like a pillbug after it is removed, but will relax again in seawater.

All chitons are bilaterally symmetrical — if you cut one in half, the halves would match. Chitons are flattened and oval or elongate. The back of the shell is slightly arched. The shell may be white, pink, aqua, or deep blue.

Chitons have a head and a mouth with radular teeth, and a powerful foot with a broad creeping sole that extends from one end of the animal to the other. They also have a simple digestive system with an anus at the rear, a pair of kidneys, a heart, gills

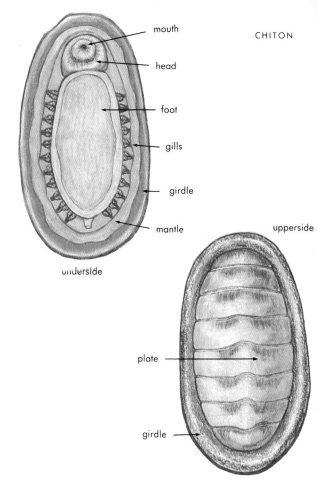

mouth

head

foot

gills

girdle

mantle

upperside

underside

plate

girdle

on either side of the body, and a nervous system.

A chiton's shell has microscopic pores containing nerves that, in some species, end in light-sensitive "eyes." Chitons can see only differences between light and dark, not distinct images.

CHITONS

WEST INDIAN CHITON 1¼–3¼ in.
The girdle is smooth and scaly, and varies in color from gray-green to a greenish brown. This chiton is found in the intertidal zone, from southern Florida to the West Indies.

BLACK KATY CHITON 1½–3 in.
Each plate has a deep diagonal groove, concealed by a smooth black girdle. The shell interior is white; the foot is reddish. This chiton is found below the low-tide line, from Alaska to California.

RED NORTHERN CHITON ½–1 in.
This chiton has a granular girdle. The shell underneath is bright pink; its upper surface is smooth except for growth wrinkles. This chiton is found just below the low-tide line or in water to 450 ft. deep, from the Arctic to Connecticut, and from Alaska to Monterey, California.

VEILED PACIFIC CHITON 1–2 in.
This chiton has a hair-studded girdle with a flap at one end that can be raised and snapped down quickly to trap prey. The shell interior is white. This chiton is found intertidally in California.

WEST INDIAN
CHITON

BLACK
KATY
CHITON

RED
NORTHERN
CHITON

VEILED
PACIFIC
CHITON

BIVALVES (PELECYPODS)

This group is the second largest group of mollusks, with about 20,000 species world-wide. Fossils of these shells have been found that date back 7500 million years.

Bivalves are two-shelled mollusks. The 2 shells are joined by interlocking teeth and are held together by an elastic ligament, which is located on the hinge. This hinge, along with one or more muscles that hold the animal in place inside its pair of shells, allows the shells to open and close. In some species both shells, or valves, are the same; in others they differ: for example, the lower (right) valve may be cupped, while the upper (left) valve is flat. Bivalve shells may vary in size, shape, thickness, sculpture, and color. As each individual grows, its original tiny shell becomes a part of the full-grown shell and is called the umbo, or "beak."

Most bivalves push themselves along with a thick muscular foot. The word pelecypod means "hachet-footed," and refers to the shape of the foot in these mollusks. Bivalves also use their foot to burrow in sand or mud.

Some bivalves seldom or never move — they glue themselves to solid surfaces or fasten themselves to rocks and other hard objects with silky threads called the byssus. A few species, the piddocks (see p. 104), bore into solids. Other bivalves swim by opening and closing their shells quickly, forcing out water and moving forward by jet propulsion.

Some bivalves, such as scallops, have nerves that end in light-sensitive eyes on the edge of the mantle. As in univalves (single-shelled snails), the fleshy mantle lines the shells and is the organ which secretes the limy substance that hardens to make the shells. In some bivalves, a part of the mantle is rolled into a pair of tubes that serve as siphons. An inhalant siphon draws in seawater, which contains oxygen and food particles. The exhalant siphon carries out excess water and body wastes. Siphons are long in clams that burrow.

All bivalves have a heart, nervous system, and digestive system. Unlike gastropods and chitons (the 2 previous groups of mollusks), bivalves have no head and no radular teeth, just a mouth opening. They filter food, algae, out of the water with their gills

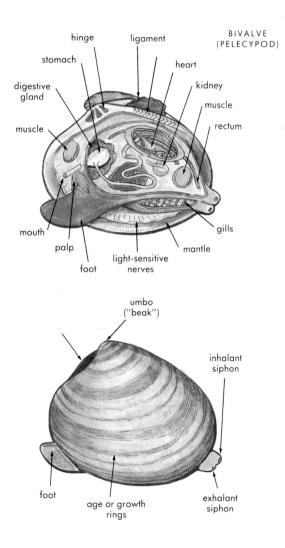

BIVALVE
(PELECYPOD)

hinge
ligament
stomach
heart
digestive gland
kidney
muscle
muscle
rectum
mouth
gills
palp
mantle
foot
light-sensitive nerves

umbo ("beak")

inhalant siphon

foot

exhalant siphon

age or growth rings

BIVALVES: SCALLOPS

There are 350 species worldwide; 65 kinds of scallops are found in North American waters.

Scallop shells are fan-shaped, with radiating lines. Some scallop shells have ridges or even knobs; others are smooth. A scallop's paired shells are usually unequal — the lower, or "right" valve, which is cupped (the one on which the animal sits when it is resting), is usually larger and duller in color than the upper, or "left" valve, which is flattened. An elastic, more-or-less triangular button, located inside the shell at the hinge line, helps keep the paired shells open, acting against the strong muscle that keeps them closed. The *"ears,"* or *wings,* of each shell vary in size. A *byssus notch* — a slender opening where the animal's anchoring threads can emerge — is found under the right ear of the shell, hinge-side up.

The animal inside each pair of scallop shells has a row of fine tentacles, and tiny, well-developed eyes fringing the outer edge of the mantle, which lines both shells.

To avoid predators, adult scallops rapidly open and close their shells with a large muscle, forcing out a rush of water that jet-propels them with explosive force, causing them to "swim" haphazardly. This muscle is the part we eat and is quite delicious.

See also p. 82.

GIANT PACIFIC SCALLOP 6–11 in.
The largest living scallop. Found in deep water, from Alaska to California.

PACIFIC PINK SCALLOP 2–3¼ in.
Found living among sponges in moderately deep water, from Alaska to southern California.

ATLANTIC DEEP-SEA SCALLOP 2–8 in.
This is the scallop that is most commonly fished and eaten in the U.S. The shell, which is almost smooth, is 2 to 8 in. high. It is found in deep water, from Canada to North Carolina.

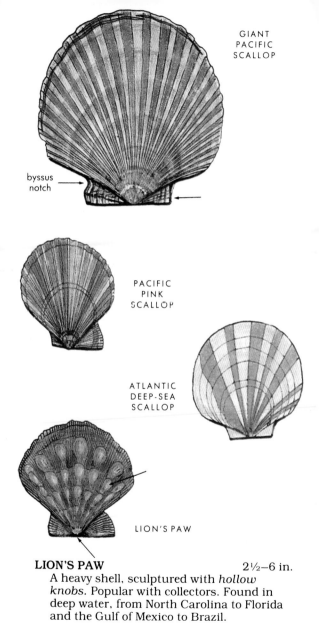

GIANT
PACIFIC
SCALLOP

byssus
notch

PACIFIC
PINK
SCALLOP

ATLANTIC
DEEP-SEA
SCALLOP

LION'S PAW

LION'S PAW   2½–6 in.
A heavy shell, sculptured with *hollow knobs*. Popular with collectors. Found in deep water, from North Carolina to Florida and the Gulf of Mexico to Brazil.

81

BIVALVES: SCALLOPS, *continued*

This is the shell shape we are most familiar with; we can see it in our surroundings on a daily basis. Since early history, artists, architects, and designers have been intrigued and inspired by the simple, elegant, and pure lines of the scallop.

THISTLE SCALLOP   ½–1½ in.
This shell is rough and thorny, like a thistle. It comes in a variety of shades of colors, mottled with white "flying bird" shapes. It is found on sand among seagrass in water 10 to 150 ft. deep, from South Carolina to South America.

SENTIS SCALLOP   1–1⅝ in.
This scaly scallop may be brightly colored or mottled. It is found on the undersides of rocks in water 1 to 500 ft. deep, from North Carolina to southeastern Florida and South America.

ICELAND SCALLOP   1¾–4 in.
This scaly shell varies in color. It is fished commercially in Greenland and Iceland, and is found in water 6 to 1000 ft. deep, from the Arctic to Massachusetts and from Alaska to Washington.

HIND'S SCALLOP   1–2½ in.
This scallop varies in color from pastels to dark reds, or spotted with white. It is found among sponges in water 1 to 600 ft. deep, from Alaska to California.

CALICO SCALLOP   1–2¾ in.
This is the commonest of the brightly colored shells found on our Atlantic beaches. It comes in many color combinations and has marked growth lines. Calico Scallops are found on sand in water 5 to 300 ft. deep. They are fished for food from North Carolina to eastern Florida.

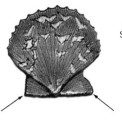

THISTLE
SCALLOP

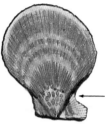

SENTIS
SCALLOP

ICELAND
SCALLOP

HIND'S
SCALLOP

CALICO
SCALLOP

BIVALVES: ARK SHELLS

This group includes approximately 200 species found worldwide in warm and temperate seas. Twenty-three are found in North American waters, mostly on the Atlantic Coast. The shape of these rigid, sturdy shells may be oval, oblong, rectangular, or even round. The shells are heavily ribbed with sculptured radiating lines; some have intersecting concentric lines.

Most arks have a prominent projection called the *"ear,"* and a *long straight hinge* with a row of many fine tiny teeth on both valves (paired shells). There is a wide elastic ligament between the hooked beaks. Some have a *gape* (opening) between the lower shells which allows the byssus threads to come through. Some arks use these threads to anchor themselves to rocks and coral. Others crawl about or burrow in sand or mud, although they have no siphon.

Arks usually have a white shell that is beautifully camouflaged with a velvety periostracum (skin). This skin can be green, brown, or black, hairy or bristly. When lying on the bottom in shallow water, ark shells look like mossy stones. Arks are used for bait and food in the Caribbean.

EARED ARK   1½–3½ in.
This ark has no byssus as an adult. It is found in mud or sand and on grasses in shallow water, from North Carolina to Brazil.

TURKEY WING   1¾–3½ in.
Found in rock crevices in shallow to deep water, from North Carolina to Brazil.

BLOOD ARK   1⅛–3 in.
Unlike most mollusks, this ark has red blood that contains hemoglobin. A cold-water ark, found in mud or sand in shallow to deep water, from Massachusetts to Brazil.

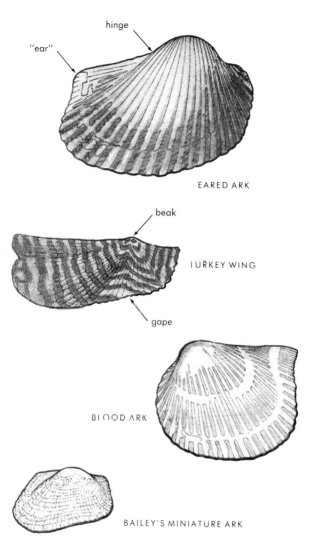

hinge

"ear"

EARED ARK

beak

TURKEY WING

gape

BLOOD ARK

BAILEY'S MINIATURE ARK

BAILEY'S MINIATURE ARK   ¼–⅜ in.
Found under stones at low-tide line, from
Baja California to the Gulf of California.

BIVALVES: LUCINES

Lucine shells are a tropical and subtropical family of about 200 species worldwide, 35 of which are found in American waters. These solid circular shells are strong but vary in thickness. The paired shells are about equal in size. The exterior is usually whitish. The elongated ligament that holds the shells together is external. The hinge may have teeth or be smooth. A *long, narrow muscle scar* at or near the front of the shell shows where the mollusk was attached to its shell.

Almost all lucines live in sand or mud, in shallow to deep water. The lucine uses its long, wormlike foot to make a mucus-lined hole in the bottom. This hole serves as an inhalant tube through which the lucine draws water and food. A very long exhalant siphon, which takes out water and wastes, can be pulled up inside the pair of shells, much like a glove with the fingers turned inside out.

TIGER LUCINE   2–3¾ in.
Our largest lucine. Intersecting lines give this bivalve's thick shells a sculptured, beaded effect. This lucine is found from southern Florida to Brazil.

BUTTERCUP LUCINE   1¼–2½ in.
A fairly thin shell with fine concentric growth lines and wrinkles. There are no teeth on the hinge. This lucine is found from North Carolina to the Caribbean.

CROSS-HATCHED LUCINE   ⅜–1 in.
A strong, inflated shell with chevronlike lines. Found from Massachusetts to Brazil.

LOVELY MINIATURE LUCINE   ¼–⅜ in.
A small thick shell with 8 or more ribs, crossed with deep, wavy concentric lines. This lucine is found from Virginia to the Bahamas and the Gulf of Mexico.

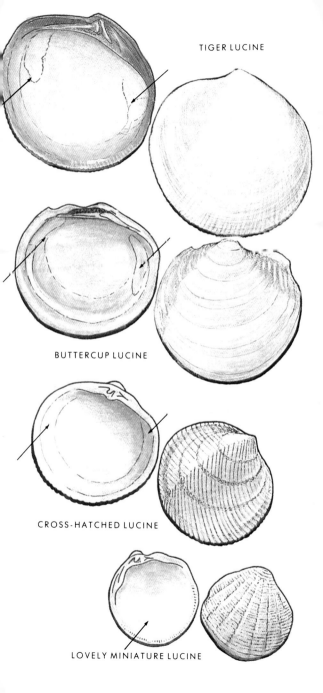

TIGER LUCINE

BUTTERCUP LUCINE

CROSS-HATCHED LUCINE

LOVELY MINIATURE LUCINE

BIVALVES: TELLIN SHELLS

There are approximately 350 species in this large tropical family. Eighty-four are native to the warmer waters off our coasts, in shallow to deep water. The tellins with thinner shells live below the surface in mud and sand, those with thicker shells in gravel.

Tellin shells are mostly elongate and flattened. They may have fine or chiseled concentric lines or be smooth. The paired shells are held together by an external ligament and a weak hinge with 2 cardinal or central teeth. Both shells are usually equal in size. There is a *slight twist* to the hind end of each shell.

The hatchet-shaped foot, which projects from one end of the paired shells, allows the tellin to burrow, or to travel hastily from side to side under sand. At the other end are 2 siphons: one long one that sweeps the bottom for rotting algae, and another that carries water and waste out of the body.

These colorful, glistening shells are used in jewelry.

ROSE-PETAL TELLIN ⅝–1½ in.
A sturdy and slightly inflated shell; it may be white as well as pink. This tellin is found from northern Florida to Brazil.

SUNRISE TELLIN 2–4 in.
Interior yellow, with rays showing through. A thin, strong, glistening shell, found from South Carolina to South America.

SALMON TELLIN ½–¾ in.
A smooth tan periostracum (skin) covers this shell. It is found from Alaska to California.

CANDY-STICK TELLIN ⅝–1⅛ in.
A thin but strong opaque shell. Found from North Carolina to Brazil.

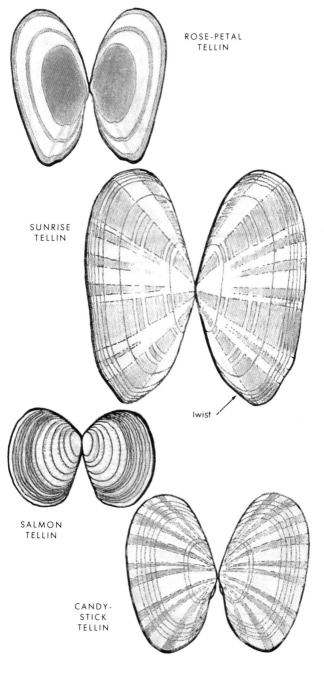

ROSE-PETAL TELLIN

SUNRISE TELLIN

Twist

SALMON TELLIN

CANDY-STICK TELLIN

BIVALVES: VENUS CLAMS

These hard, thick-shelled clams are found in soft seabeds. This is a large family of bivalves, with 500 species worldwide. Seventy-five species are found in warm and cold waters on both coasts of North America.

Some venus clams are colorful. Shapes range from squarish, circular, and triangular to ovate (egg-shaped) and the valves may be thick or thin. Venus clams come in many textures as well — some are sculptured with spines, ridges, and ribs; others are glassy smooth. They are equivalved, meaning both shells are the same. There are usually at least 3 central teeth on each valve. A flexible external ligament and a powerful muscle attached to the interior of the shells enable the animal to open its valves and close them to protect its soft body.

These clams lie buried a little below the surface of the bottom sediments, usually in mud. They have 2 separate, well-developed siphons that can be extended above the mud to inhale salty water filled with the minute organisms they use for food. A large, hatchet-shaped foot allows them to move about freely or to burrow.

Venus clams have been used for food since prehistoric times.

See also p. 96.

CROSS-BARRED VENUS   To 1¾ in.
Found in North Carolina to Brazil.

KING VENUS   1½–2 in.
Found from southern Florida to the West Indies.

RIBBED VENUS   To 1½ in.
An unusual-looking shell. Found in California.

ELEGANT VENUS   To 2 in.
(ROYAL COMB SHELL)
Uncommon. Found from Texas to the Caribbean.

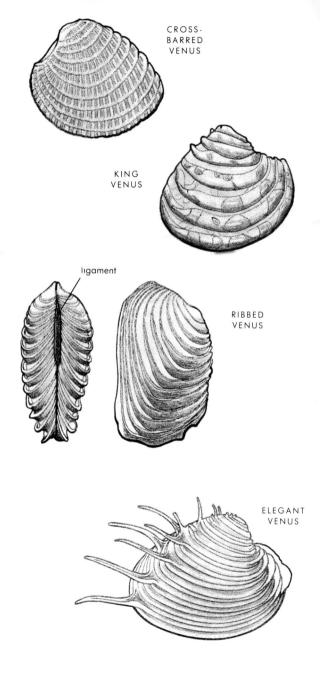

CROSS-BARRED VENUS

KING VENUS

ligament

RIBBED VENUS

ELEGANT VENUS

BIVALVES:
VENUS CLAMS, *continued*

NORTHERN QUAHOG $1\frac{1}{2}-4\frac{1}{2}$ in.
This is the most important edible bivalve sold along the East Coast. Other names for this clam are cherrystone, little neck, round clam, and hard-shelled clam. The commercial names are based on shell sizes: cherrystones are 2 in. long, little necks $1\frac{1}{2}$ in. long, and chowder size 3 in. long.

The Algonquin Indians of New England called this clam the quahog or quahaug. These are the shells that Indian money, or "wampum," was made from. Of particular value was the money made from the purple spot near the hind end, on the inside of each shell.

PISMO CLAM $2\frac{1}{2}-6\frac{1}{4}$ in.
An important and delicious food clam in California. Commercial digging is not allowed. Each digger's catch is limited to 15 clams, not less than 5 in. long, per day. The interior of the shell is cream-colored.

This clam is found from California to Mexico.

POINTED VENUS $\frac{1}{2}-1$ in.
The interior can be shades of white, brown, or purple. Found from southern Florida to Texas and south to Mexico.

LIGHTNING VENUS $1-2$ in.
Named because of the lightning-flash designs on the shell. Found from North Carolina to Brazil.

GLORY-OF-THE-SEAS VENUS To 1 in.
A rare shell, somewhat thinner than other venus clams. Found by dredging or in fish stomachs, from North Carolina to Texas in deep water.

NORTHERN
QUAHOG

PISMO
CLAM

POINTED
VENUS

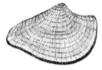

LIGHTNING
VENUS

GLORY-OF-
THE-SEAS
VENUS

BIVALVES: GAPER CLAMS

There are 20 or more mostly northern species worldwide. Ten are found in our cooler North American waters.

A thin *periostracum* (skin) covers these thin, chalky white shells. The shells are usually elongate or ovate (egg-shaped), open at both ends or the hind end, and are not able to close completely. The hinge has no teeth. *The left valve has a shelf* that projects and holds the internal ligament. This shelf fits together with a parallel indentation in the right valve. The clam has a long, retractable siphon covered by a tough skin tube.

Gaper clams burrow in mud or sand, or live in holes in clay or soft rock. You can find them at low tide by watching for little squirts of water above the sand.

SOFT-SHELLED CLAM   1–5½ in.
(STEAMER, GAPER, OR MANINOSE)

This delicious clam is dredged commercially. It is found in sand or mud, from arctic seas to North Carolina, and from British Columbia to central California.

CHUBBY MYA   1¾–3 in.

This clam lives in sand, clay, or shale. It is found from British Columbia to lower California.

GEODUCK   3½–9 in.

This thick, hard-shelled clam has a small foot, but burrows into the sandy mud with the sheer weight of its body and massive snout. A geoduck cannot withdraw its siphon any more than ⅔ of its total length, but the siphon can extend as much as 4 ft. to clear water.

American Indians called the mollusks gweducks ("gooey-ducks"). These clams are tough but delicious to eat. They are found on beaches at very low tides, from southern Alaska to Baja California.

SOFT-SHELLED CLAM

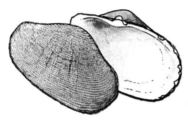

CHUBBY MYA

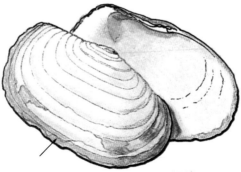

GEODUCK

BIVALVES: SANGUIN CLAMS

The color patterns of these clams range from striking to dull. The paired shells are longish, oval, rounded, and unequal — the left valve (shell) is inflated and the right one flattened. The *external ligament* is mounted on a shell platform at the top of the hinge on the left valve. The shells have small hinge teeth and are slightly open at the end to accommodate the clam's separate and extremely long siphons. The *large, U-shaped mark* inside the shell, which shows where the siphon-retracting muscles were attached, is called the pallial sinus. Another *scar* inside the shell, which shows where the mantle muscles were attached, is called the pallial line.

Sanguin clams are rapid burrowers and live in mud, sandy mud, or gravel. They are found intertidally in warm seas, and in brackish, shallow muddy water in the tropics. Many of these clams are edible, and they are fished commercially in Asia.

ATLANTIC SANGUIN   1½–2 in.
A smooth glossy shell. Found in sandy mud, from southern Florida and the Gulf states to the West Indies.

NUTTALL'S MAHOGANY CLAM   2½–3¾ in.
A shiny, nut brown, tough periostracum (skin) covers this blue shell with purple rays. It is common in bays and near estuaries, usually buried in 6 to 8 in. of mud, from southern California to Baja California.

GAUDY ASAPHIS   1½–2½ in.
Both the color rays on the shell's sculptured exterior and the glossy interior are a variety of lovely colors. This clam is found in gravel intertidally, from southeastern Florida to the West Indies and also in the Indo-Pacific.

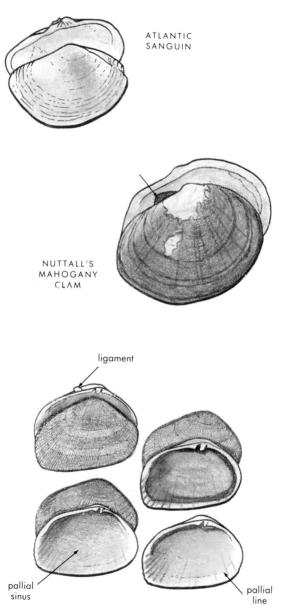

ATLANTIC SANGUIN

NUTTALL'S MAHOGANY CLAM

ligament

pallial sinus

pallial line

GAUDY ASAPHIS

BIVALVES: RAZOR CLAMS

There are 100 species distributed in seas worldwide; 13 in our coastal waters. Most razor clams are edible.

The edges of these clams are razor-sharp. Both shells are equal in size and oblong or elongate but slightly oval in shape. (They can be 2 to 6 times as long as they are wide.) Each shell is strengthened by a *raised rib inside.* The outside of the shell is smooth except for growth lines, and is covered by a periostracum. The narrow ligament that holds the shells together is external. The *hinge is off center,* toward the front end. The central teeth on each shell are few and vary in number.

Razor clams are slightly open at both ends. A strong muscular foot enables these clams to burrow with incredible speed to escape their foes. Fully extended, the foot is as long as the shell. To retreat into the sand, the clam assumes a vertical position and thrusts the foot downward. The foot swells and then contracts, drawing the shell into the mud or sand. This curved, powerful foot allows some razor clams to move easily along the bottom. The clam folds its foot back tightly against the shell like a coiled spring and then suddenly lets it go, which propels the clam forward. When this process is rapidly repeated, the clam zigzags quickly out of sight.

ATLANTIC RAZOR CLAM   1½–2⅝ in.
Found from Canada to North Carolina.

PACIFIC RAZOR CLAM   3–6¼ in.
This commercially fished clam is found from Alaska to California.

TRANSPARENT RAZOR CLAM   1–1½ in.
Found from central California to Baja California.

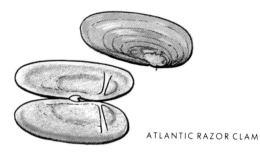

ATLANTIC RAZOR CLAM

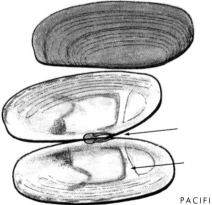

PACIFIC RAZOR CLAM

TRANSPARENT RAZOR CLAM

BIVALVES: PIDDOCK SHELLS

Piddock shells live in the warmer waters of all seas. Of 92 species, 24 are in our area.

From the delicate perfection of these thin white shells, one would never guess that the living animal can bore up to 3 ft. into hard materials such as clay, peat, wood, cement, coral, plastic, lead, shale, and rock. The outer shell, especially on the hind end, has a raspy texture that is sharp and abrasive. With the aid of its powerful adductor muscle and suction foot, a piddock rocks back and forth, twisting and turning, flushing away debris with jets of water, until it has bored a burrow where it will live. Piddocks can be very destructive.

A piddock shell is widely agape (open) at both ends. The top margin of the shell folds back on itself. Foot muscles are attached to a *shelly projection* inside the shell. A special plate made of limy shell material partially surrounds the base of the siphon and protects the muscle that holds the 2 shells together. The siphon, encased in a rough tubular sheath, may extend 2 or 3 times the length of the shell, but does not retract completely. The shell has a thin gray periostracum.

Piddocks are edible.

ANGEL WING   4–8 in.
A rare pink piddock. Found in sticky mud, from Massachusetts to Brazil.

CAMPECHE ANGEL WING   2–4¾ in.
This shell has *shelly reinforcements* under its *rolled margin.* This piddock is found from North Carolina to Brazil.

FALLEN ANGEL WING   1¼–2¾ in.
Found in mud or shale, from Maine to Brazil.

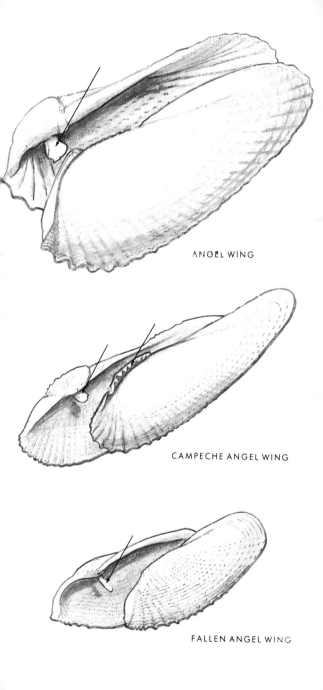

ANGEL WING

CAMPECHE ANGEL WING

FALLEN ANGEL WING

BIVALVES: MUSSELS

Of the 250 species found all over the world,
55 live along the coasts of North America.
Mussels grow best in cool waters. Under
ideal conditions a mussel may reach full
growth in a year, but maturity sometimes
takes 2 to 5 years.

Mussels have a pair of thin, equal-sized
shells. They may be oval, oblong, elongate,
and curved in shape, and are usually
sharply pointed at the *umbo* ("beak") on the
front end. A tan or blue-black *periostracum*
(skin) covers the outer shell. Microscopic
layers of limy material (mother-of-pearl) give
the inside of the shell its iridescent rainbow
colors, which are like the prism effect of the
sun shining through a drop of water. The
ligament that holds the shells together is
inside the shell and sits on a shelf behind
the umbones. The hinge is smooth or has
one or more small teeth. There are 2 muscle
scars inside the shell — a small one in front
and a large one in the rear.

See also p. 108.

NORTHERN HORSE MUSSEL   2–9 in.
This mussel is not eaten here, but it is in
some parts of Europe. Found among gravel
or rocks, from the Arctic to New York.

SAY'S CHESTNUT MUSSEL   ¾–1½ in.
Found in sand or mud among seagrass,
from South Carolina to the West Indies.

BLUE MUSSEL   1¼–4 in.
This delicious mussel has been used as food
here, but is more popular in Europe. Common and widespread; found on rocks and
pilings, from the Arctic to South Carolina
and in California.

CALIFORNIA MUSSEL   2–10 in.
The largest mussel. This edible mussel is a
veritable untapped source of nutrition.

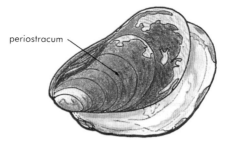

periostracum

NORTHERN HORSE MUSSEL

BLUE MUSSEL

SAY'S CHESTNUT MUSSEL

umbo ("beak")

CALIFORNIA MUSSEL

BIVALVES: MUSSELS, *continued*

Mussels live in dense colonies, often in large banks. Some mussels live in the open and hold fast to roots, shells, rocks, and pilings. Others cling to old burrows in clay, wood, coral, and rock. Date mussels can burrow with their long, slender foot. They can secrete an acid that helps them make new holes in soft rock that will fit their shells exactly.

All mussels secrete a *byssus*, a bundle of sticky, hairlike threads that harden rapidly. The byssus is used by the mussel to moor itself to any foundation available. Although we find it almost impossible to sever these tough silky threads, the animal can break them at will. By using its foot, it can move to another place, where it spins a new byssus and anchors itself.

Many mussels are delicious to eat, but when they feed on toxic algae they can become poisonous.

SCORCHED MUSSEL ⅝–1⅝ in.
The front edge of the shell is smooth, but there are 2 to 4 teeth under the umbones (beaks). This mussel is found on rocks and pilings, from North Carolina to Brazil.

TULIP MUSSEL 1¼–4 in.
This red shell has a brown periostracum. It is found on broken shells and moss-covered rocks, from South Carolina to Brazil.

HOOKED MUSSEL 1–2⅜ in.
There are 2 or 4 teeth on the shell below the umbones. This mussel is found on oyster beds and pilings, from Maryland to the West Indies.

YELLOW MUSSEL ⅞–1⅝ in.
There are 3 to 4 teeth below the umbones, and small teeth on the edge of the shell. This mussel is found on rocks, from southern Florida to the West Indies.

SCORCHED
MUSSEL

TULIP
MUSSEL

HOOKED
MUSSEL

YELLOW
MUSSEL

BIVALVES: PEN SHELLS

There are 20 species of pens worldwide. Pen shells live in colonies, in warm shallow water to moderately deep seas. Some live in quiet bays and tidepools. We have 4 species along the southern part of our East Coast and 1 rare black species in California.

Pen shells are usually shaped like a triangle that is longer than it is wide, similar to a half-open fan. The shell gapes at the wide posterior (rear) end. It can be smooth or covered with fine teeth or spines. The outside is rough and dull, but the inside is smooth and has a pearly iridescence extending from the pointed tip through the muscle scar. The shell is large and is made of layers of large, prismatic crystals that make it brittle and fragile. There is a narrow ligament that holds the pair of shells together. The hinge has no teeth.

A small muscular foot spins the byssus, a strong bundle of silky anchor threads with a metallic glow. The threads emerge from the pointed end of the shell, known as the *umbonal tip*, or *apex*. Cloth woven from a golden byssus is said to be the finest and most costly in the world. It is thought to be the "golden fleece" sought by Jason in Greek mythology.

Pen shells burrow in soft sand or sandy mud, apex down, and attach themselves to shell fragments or stones with their byssus. The sharp, broad hind end of the shell, which sticks out of the sand an inch or so, can hurt a wader's bare foot. In the soft parts of the animal there is a gutterlike waste canal and a finger-shaped pallial organ (produced by the mantle) that is used to remove broken shells and unused food. Crabs and shrimps living in the mantle cavity eat any leftovers that are not ejected by this special organ. Mollusks sometimes fasten themselves to the shell's exterior.

Sea pens produce lustrous red, orange, and black pearls that have no commercial value. The large muscle inside a pen shell is eaten, like a scallop.

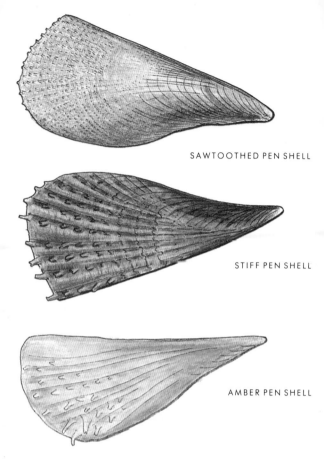

SAWTOOTHED PEN SHELL

STIFF PEN SHELL

AMBER PEN SHELL

SAWTOOTHED PEN SHELL　　　6–12 in.
Found from North Carolina to Texas and
South America.

STIFF PEN SHELL　　　5–11 in.
Found from North Carolina to the Caribbean.

AMBER PEN SHELL　　　4–11 in.
A weak groove runs down the middle of
each translucent valve. Found from southeastern Florida to the Caribbean.

BIVALVES: THORNY OYSTERS

These highly collectible shells are also known as chrysanthemum shells. Forty species or more are found worldwide, in shallow to deep water and in all tropical seas. We have 2 species on each of our coasts.

Thorny oyster shells come in an assortment of beautiful colors: some are white with tinted *umbones (beaks)*; others are varying shades of the same color or one intense color. The shell exterior is sculptured with radiating ribs that may be ruffled or ornamented with scale-like shelly formations, or armed with spines. The spines may be long or short, blunt or pointed, and may be cupped or curled. Flawless specimens with long beautiful spines are found in deep quiet water, while ones that wash up on the beach are usually badly worn.

These bivalves use their right or lower valve to attach themselves permanently to rocks, coral reefs, sea walls, and sunken wrecks. Crowded conditions often produce irregularly shaped specimens. Thorny oysters have light-sensitive eyes along the mantle and are more closely related to scallops than to the oysters we eat.

The paired shells of thorny oysters are thick but unequal in size. The ligament that holds the shells together is found in the *broad, triangular hinge area*, in a hole between the 2 interlocking "ball-and-socket" hinge teeth. The teeth fit together so perfectly that it is almost impossible to separate the shells without fracturing them.

PACIFIC THORNY OYSTER   1½–6 in.

The spines, usually less than 1½ in. long, are curved or bent. This oyster comes in a wide range of brilliant colors; sometimes it is white. It is found in deep water, from the Gulf of California to Ecuador.

PACIFIC THORNY OYSTER

"beak"

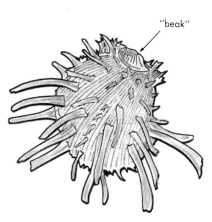

ATLANTIC THORNY OYSTER

ATLANTIC THORNY OYSTER 1½–8 in.
The spines are 3 in. long. Colors vary from
white (tinted with other colors) to one solid
color. This oyster is found from North Carolina to Brazil.

113

BIVALVES: JEWEL-BOX SHELLS

These shells vary in size, form, and color. There are more than 20 tropical species worldwide; 13 are found in North America. Jewel-box shells are usually found living permanently cemented to shells, sturdy plants, sea walls, rocks, coral, and sunken wrecks, in shallow to extremely deep water.

Jewel-box shells are white or a delicate pastel color. These medium-sized, thick shells are oval to roundish or irregularly formed. The outer surface may be frilly, leafy, or spiny; it may have rows of flattened, plate-like or blade-like spines. Jewel boxes that live in calm deep water are more vividly colored and their shelly fronds may grow to be long and perfect. The shell interior is white and, in some, china-like.

These mollusks may attach themselves to a hard surface with either their left or right valve (shell). When they cling to a surface with their left valve, their umbones (beaks) shift from right to left, and when they fasten down their right valve, the umbones turn from left to right. Jewel boxes attach themselves very firmly to their home spot. They are not easy to spot, because they are covered with algae and other mollusks.

The ligament that holds the shells together is external, and there is a strong thick hinge, usually with one main tooth. *The umbones turn forward.* In a living jewel box, the edges of the animal's mantle have colorful extensions.

Excavations of mounds of Indian relics have turned up these shells, indicating that they were used as food hundreds of years ago.

CLEAR JEWEL BOX　　　　　　　1½–3⅓ in.
Found from Oregon to Chile.

LEAFY JEWEL BOX　　　　　　　1¼–3½ in.
Found from Florida to Brazil.

FLORIDA SPINY JEWEL BOX　　　1–2½ in.
Adults are found unattached, from North Carolina to Mexico.

CLEAR JEWEL BOX

LEAFY JEWEL BOX

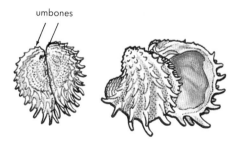

umbones

FLORIDA SPINY JEWEL BOX

BIVALVES: JINGLE SHELLS

There are 25 species worldwide. Seven of them are common within our range, in shallow to deep warm water.

The thin valves (paired halves) of a jingle shell are usually rounded or irregular in shape, and unequal in size. The hinge is toothless. The interior of the *left valve*, which is cupped, is pearly. Jingles are attached permanently to rocks, seaweed, or shells by their *right valve*, which is flattened. The shell is anchored by a strong, calcified plug of a *byssus* that emerges through a *hole* in the lower shell.

COMMON JINGLE SHELL   ¾–2¼ in.
This sugary-looking, translucent shell comes in pale sherbet colors — yellows and oranges. It is found from Massachusetts to Brazil.

BIVALVES: KITTEN'S PAWS

Out of 10 species worldwide, 5 are found intertidally in North America. Kitten's paws cement themselves to shells or rocks; either valve (shell) may be the base. There are interlocking ball-and-socket teeth on the hinge inside the valves, on either side of the ligament pit.

KITTEN'S PAW   To ¾ in.
Found from North Carolina to the West Indies.

BIVALVES: WING OYSTERS

Of about 20 species worldwide, 5 are found in our warm seas, on rocks, shells, and plants. This family includes the pearl oysters. Wing oysters are not palatable.

These oyster shells are moderately thick, but thin on the outer edges. Each has a strong byssus, a periostracum, and a lovely mother-of-pearl interior.

ATLANTIC WING OYSTER   1½–3½ in.
Found from North Carolina to Brazil.

WESTERN WING OYSTER   3–4 in.
Found from California to Canada.

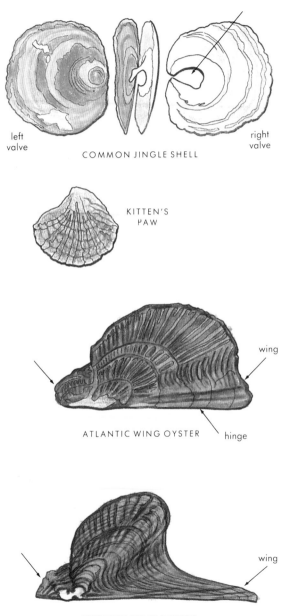

left valve

right valve

COMMON JINGLE SHELL

KITTEN'S PAW

ATLANTIC WING OYSTER

wing

hinge

WESTERN WING OYSTER

wing

BIVALVES: OYSTERS

Oysters are the most valuable of all the food mollusks. They are found in shallow water worldwide, except in the Arctic and the Antarctic. Of the 50 species in this group, 8 live in our North American waters.

Oysters are commonly elongate, but can be circular or very irregular in shape. Oyster shells are medium-sized to large and heavy. They are generally a dull gray or drab color but may have color rays. The exterior is relatively smooth except for growth lines and occasional flutes. The interior is smooth, shiny, and porcelain-like. Equivalve oysters (those with matching shell halves) have interiors that are colorful, with a colorless muscle scar. Inequivalves are white inside, with a *muscle scar* that is a purplish red or blue. In oysters there is one adductor muscle; the muscle scar is visible on both valves. A triangular ligament is found in a *pit* in the center of the apex of the shell. There are no teeth on the hinge.

Oysters are hermaphroditic: they start life as a male, finish as a female, and reverse many times in between. The spat, or young, swim freely until they develop shells (within the first 24 hours) and settle down on a solid surface. They attach themselves permanently to shells, rocks, sea plants, or roots, first with their foot, then with a byssus, which they lose, and finally by their lower (left) valve, which is usually cupped. The upper (right) valve is usually flattened and slightly smaller.

These tasty bivalves are eaten by humans, crabs, fishes, birds, worms, starfishes, sponges, and predatory snails called oyster drills, but the biggest threats to their survival are diseases, fungi, parasites, and pollution.

Oysters need certain conditions in order to survive. They prefer water that is salty, but not too salty. They are gathered with hand and mechanical tongs and dredges, and by skin divers, on natural oyster beds or seeded beds.

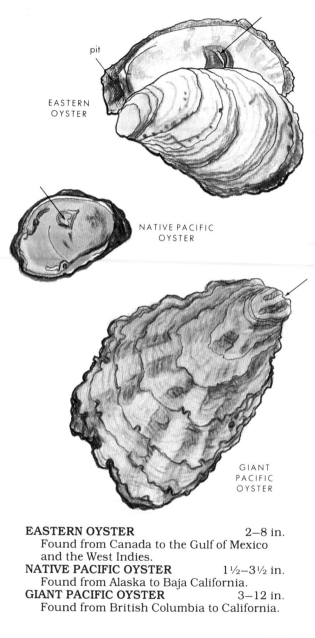

pit

EASTERN
OYSTER

NATIVE PACIFIC
OYSTER

GIANT
PACIFIC
OYSTER

EASTERN OYSTER   2–8 in.
  Found from Canada to the Gulf of Mexico
  and the West Indies.
NATIVE PACIFIC OYSTER   1½–3½ in.
  Found from Alaska to Baja California.
GIANT PACIFIC OYSTER   3–12 in.
  Found from British Columbia to California.

SCAPHOPODS
(TUSK SHELLS AND OTHERS)

The word scaphopod means "plow foot." These shells have been in existence for 300 million years. The 2 families in this group, the tusk and cadulus shells, contain about 1000 species distributed worldwide. They live in marine waters ranging from 10 ft. to 3 miles deep.

We have about 200 species in North America. They range in size from a small, needle-thin shell on ½ in. long to one that is 5 in. long. Scaphopods "grow" by adding thin layers of shell material, manufactured by the mantle, to the larger end of the shell.

A cadulus shell is open at both ends but swollen in the middle, and has a wormlike foot that flares out into a disk on the end (see p. 121).

Tusk shells are hollow — they are shaped like an elephant's tusk and are open at both ends. These slender, symmetrical, tapering tubes can be straight or curved and sometimes have a slit or notch at the small end.

Tusks dig into sand or mud with a long, elastic, cone-shaped foot and lie buried at an angle, large end down. The foot emerges from this lower end, along with several prehensile filaments with club-shaped ends. These filaments, which are attached to lobes around the mouth, branch out under the sand to anchor the tusk shell and capture food — single-celled protozoa — and pass it to the tusk animal's mouth, where it is crushed with the radular teeth and then digested. The filaments grow back if severed.

The apex, or small end, of a tusk shell sticks out of the sand into the water. Water is sucked into this small end and enters the mantle cavity, where it stays (for about 10 minutes) until oxygen is absorbed from the water by tissues in the mantle. Colorless blood is circulated. Food is also brought in with the water and wastes are taken out as the water is expelled back through the apex. This system is so efficient that the tusk has no tentacles, eyes, head, gills, or heart; it has no need for them. Sexes are separate.

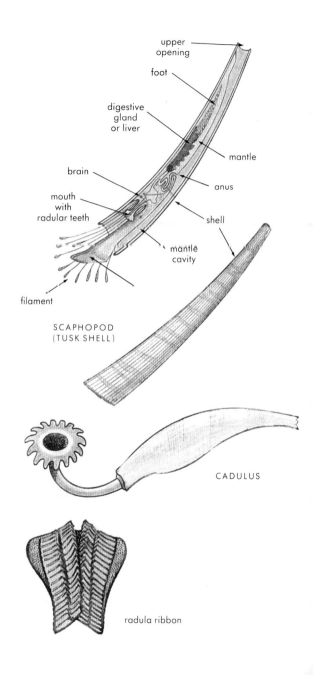

upper opening

foot

digestive gland or liver

mantle

brain

anus

mouth with radular teeth

shell

filament

mantle cavity

SCAPHOPOD
(TUSK SHELL)

CADULUS

radula ribbon

SCAPHOPODS: TUSK SHELLS

There are 40 species of North American tusks. They are found buried in sand, in shallow to deep water.

Tusk shells are usually white, but may have delicate tints of yellow or pink. In the East Indies, the colors of these shells can be intense, bright greens. Tusk shells are often smooth, but some have fine lengthwise ridges and others have encircling lines. In cross section, the shells are round, elliptical, octagonal, hexagonal, or polygonal. The interior may be porcelain-like or dull and chalky.

Enemies of tusks include crabs and fish. Pacific Indians used tusks as wampum or money; the value of the shells varied with their size. Tusk shells were also used in necklaces and other forms of ornamentation. A tribal costume adorned with tusks was a real display of wealth.

INDIAN MONEY TUSK   1–2½ in.
This is the tusk the Indians usually used for money. It is a white, ivory-textured shell, sometimes with yellow rings. Found from Alaska to Mexico.

FLORIDA TUSK   2¼–3 in.
A rare deep-water, hard-shelled tusk. Found from Florida to the Caribbean.

TEXAS TUSK   ¾–1¼ in.
A common deep-water, hard-shelled tusk. It is *hexagonal* in cross section (see p. 123). This tusk is found from North Carolina to the Gulf states.

IVORY TUSK   1–2 in.
A common, shiny, shallow-water tusk. Found from North Carolina to Florida, Texas, and the West Indies.

SHINING TUSK   To 2 in.
A perfectly smooth tusk. Found in the Gulf of Mexico.

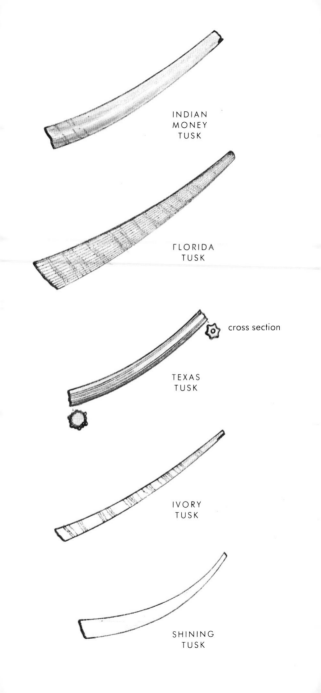

INDIAN
MONEY
TUSK

FLORIDA
TUSK

cross section

TEXAS
TUSK

IVORY
TUSK

SHINING
TUSK

CEPHALOPODS: SQUIDS, OCTOPUSES, AND OTHERS

This is a large class of mollusks, with several hundred species worldwide. This group has been in existence on earth for more than 200 million years. Cephalopods are the largest and most highly developed of all the mollusks. Their central nervous system is extremely efficient and they have excellent vision. Except for the nautiluses, which have 4 gills, cephalopods have 2 gills. They also have 2 kidneys and 3 hearts (one main heart and 2 auxiliary ones), which circulate blue blood.

Cephalopods have a soft body, which is bilaterally symmetrical. Except for the chambered nautiluses, which live in the Indo-Pacific, cephalopods have no outer shell. Members of one group — the cuttlefishes — have a shell-like blade inside the mantle cavity. This blade, which contains calcium and is called the cuttlebone, helps strengthen the animal's body. In squids, the mantle and fins are supported by a simple rod or a featherlike, horny internal shell called a pen.

The word cephalopod means "head foot." In these mollusks, the head is well developed and a ring of 8 or more arms with suction cups or hooks surrounds the mouth. Octopuses have 8 arms; the cuttlefishes and squids have 8 arms and 2 tentacles. The mouth has a parrotlike beak and radular teeth. Cephalopods are carnivores — they feed on shrimps, crabs, fishes, and other cephalopods.

All cephalopods crawl or swim actively. A muscular mantle covers the body, which in most species is built for speed. Water is drawn into the pocketlike mantle cavity and is discharged, along with wastes, through a siphon or funnel. Cephalopods swim by forcefully expelling a series of jets of water through the funnel. They shoot backward, jet propelled, tail first and arms streaming behind. By aiming the funnel, a squid or octopus can also direct its course. Squids

have a streamlined body with *fins* on either side of the tail.

Cephalopods can change color at will, blending in completely with their surroundings. They also have an ink sac that can squirt black fluid to discourage predators.

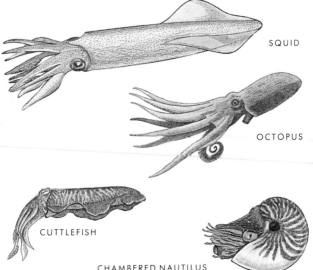

SQUID

OCTOPUS

CUTTLEFISH

CHAMBERED NAUTILUS

ARGONAUTS AND SPIRULA

The argonauts include 6 to 8 species that live in tropical or warm-temperate waters worldwide.

PAPER NAUTILUS   Female 8 in.:
(ARGONAUT)   male ½−1 in.

This octopus has prominent eyes. It is not often seen, but its empty egg cases occasionally wash up on shore. The egg case is a delicate, *unchambered*, paper-thin, calcareous "shell" (see p. 126). The female secretes the egg case from her 2 dorsal arms and holds it with those arms, which are webbed and widened. She is not attached to this "egg basket" and can leave it at will. The male is smaller than the female and

makes no shell. One of the male's arms is modified into a specialized reproductive arm called the hectocotylus (see below), which is located in a sac below the left eye. When the sac ruptures, this arm is detached from the male's body and fertilizes the spongy mass of eggs in the female's egg case.

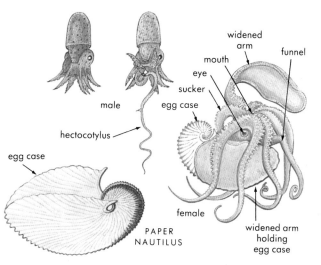

male

hectocotylus

egg case

egg case

widened arm

mouth

funnel

eye

sucker

female

widened arm holding egg case

PAPER NAUTILUS

SPIRULA
To 3 in.

This tiny, squidlike creature lives in deep waters of the Atlantic, Pacific, and Indian oceans. A small (1-in. long), hollow, coiled shell called the Ram's Horn is embedded in the rear end of the Spirula's body. This internal shell has *chambers* filled with air and gas. Spirulas have a light-producing organ at the rear of the body that gives off a constant yellow-green glow called bioluminescence. These cephalopods hang in the dimly lit depths, tail up, casting their light upward.

SPIRULA

RAM'S HORN

126

Index

Color illustrations of the shells generally appear on the page facing the text. To avoid duplication, the illustrations are not indexed separately.

127